182

P9-DIJ-266

THE ROAD TO UNAFRAID

THE ROAD TO UNAFRAID

How the Army's Top Ranger Faced Fear and Found Courage
Through "Black Hawk Down" and Beyond

CAPTAIN JEFF STRUECKER

WITH DEAN MERRILL

W PUBLISHING GROUP
A Division of Thomas Nelson Publishers
Since 1798
www.wpublishinggroup.com

Published by W Publishing Group, a Division of Thomas Nelson, Inc., P.O. Box 141000, Nashville, Tennessee, 37214.

Jeff Struecker is represented by The Nashville Agency, P.O. Box 110909, Nashville, TN 37222.

Dean Merrill is represented by Mark Sweeney & Associates, 28540 Altessa Way, Suite 201, Bonita Springs, FL 34135.

W Publishing Group books may be purchased in bulk for educational, business, fundraising, or sales promotional use. For information, please email SpecialMarkets@ThomasNelson.com.

All Scripture quotations, unless otherwise indicated, are taken from The Holy Bible, New Living Translation (NLT), copyright © 1996. Used by permission of Tyndale House Publishers, Inc., Wheaton, Illinois 60189. All rights reserved.

Other Scripture references are from the following sources:

The Holy Bible, New International Version (NIV). Copyright © 1973, 1978, 1984. International Bible Society. Used by permission of Zondervan Bible Publishers.

The New King James Version (NKJV), copyright © 1979, 1980, 1982, Thomas Nelson, Inc., Publishers.

Editorial Staff: Greg Daniel, Acquisitions Editor, and Thom Chittom, managing editor.
Cover Design: DesignPoint, Inc.
Page Design: Walter Petrie

The views presented are those of the author and do not necessarily represent the views of Department of Defense or its Components.

Library of Congress Cataloging-in-Publication Data

Struecker, Jeff, 1969–
    The road to unafraid : how the Army's top ranger faced fear and found courage through Black Hawk Down and beyond / Jeff Struecker with Dean Merrill.
        p. cm.
    ISBN-10: 0-8499-0060-3
    ISBN-13: 978-0-8499-0060-0
    1. Struecker, Jeff, 1969– 2. United States. Army—Commando troops—Biography. 3. United States. Army—Officers—Biography. 4. United States. Army—Chaplains—Biography. 5. Baptists—United States—Clergy—Biography. 6. Fear—Biblical teaching. I. Merrill, Dean. II. Title.
    U53.S778A3 2006
    355.0092—dc22
    [B]   2006012964

Printed in the United States of America

06 07 08 09 10 QW 5 4 3 2 1

To Dawn,
an awesome wife
and my best friend.

CONTENTS

Introduction: Fearless?   ix

1. A Small Problem   1

2. Questions in the Night   19

3. Into the Unknown   29

4. First Blood   49

5. Iowa Bride   63

6. Follow the Rules   83

7. Round Two   93

8. The All-Nighter   105

9. Survivors   123

10. Slap in the Face   131

11. The Best?   147

12. A Hard Right Turn   165

13. In Search of Daily Bread   175

14. On Edge   187

15. The Anchor   197

Endnotes   209

Introduction

FEARLESS?

U.S. ARMY RANGERS DON'T GET SCARED. WE'VE MADE A name for ourselves as the fearless ones. We're a tough, disciplined, quick-strike force that parachutes or helicopters into nasty situations, kicks down doors, captures the bad guys, and forces openings for the rest of the army to follow—hence our motto, "Rangers Lead the Way."

Give us the hardest, most dangerous, most challenging mission you can think of. We'll take it on. We're the elite—fewer than half a percent of all active-duty soldiers. We go where others are not able or not trained to go. We instinctively run *toward* the fight, not away from it.

At least that's the mystique. Line up any one hundred guys who have served successfully in the Ranger Regiment and ask if they've ever been afraid. You'll get no takers.

We stand in the long, proud line of those Rangers who first pushed onto Omaha Beach on D-Day back in 1944. It was Rangers who scaled straight up the ninety-foot cliffs of Pointe-du-Hoc that day to knock out a nest of 155-millimeter German cannons that were holding off the Allied invasion.

It was Rangers who jumped onto the airfields of Grenada (1983), taking on the enemy with no backup for hours. We Rangers did the same in Panama (1989). We were the ones who came oh-so-close to breaking the back of Somali warlord Mohamed Farrah Aidid and restoring sanity to that desperate country (1993)—until our government pulled us out. If you've read Mark Bowden's excellent bestseller *Black Hawk Down* or seen the Academy Award–winning movie, you know all about that. In this book, I'll give you my take on what happened there.

Along the way I may surprise you by admitting that I've been afraid more than once or twice during my thirteen-plus years in the Ranger Regiment. That may upset some people. But it's true.

I've felt the same fears as those who've never worn the uniform. Fear of death. Fear of losing your most valued relationships. Fear of running out of money. Fear of getting sick. Fear of violence. Fear of embarrassment. These happen all across the human spectrum.

How we handle our fears makes a huge difference. We can let them paralyze us, or we can find the courage to rise above them. Through my experiences, I share some extreme examples of facing threats and overcoming the panic they generate inside. My hope is to encourage you in your private battles.

A U.S. military firebase somewhere in Afghanistan during the Global War on Terrorism.

One

A Small Problem

It was a Sunday afternoon, but I can assure you nobody was taking a nap. Earlier thoughts about organizing a volley-ball game in the warm sun at our Mogadishu airport compound by the ocean were long forgotten. Intelligence was now saying we had a golden opportunity to catch not one but two high aides to Mohamed Farrah Aidid, the warlord who was basically ruining Somalia.

This desert country on the tip of northeast Africa didn't just have a bad government, it had not had a functioning government at all for the past two years. If you wanted to mail a letter, there was no postal system to accept or deliver it. If you had a child who needed school-ing, there was no such public institution. If you were in trouble and needed a police officer for protection, you'd better have a bribe ready.

It was such a shame, because as I had looked around Mogadishu, I couldn't help thinking it had the potential to be one of the world's great resort cities. The gentle breezes off the Indian Ocean, the sandy beaches, the warm sunshine—it all compared to the French Riviera. Instead, it was currently shot to pieces, totally trashed, the most violent place on earth. Only the mosques seemed to have been spared.

Aidid and his competitors ran daily life through sheer force, controlling the drug trade and choking off the world's food aid as soon as it arrived in the port. He had a sinister scheme for getting and keeping fighters. His policy was simple: free drugs if you'll join my militia. As a result, he had recruited thousands of desperate young men who stayed high much of the time. The average Somali lived in daily fear—more than two million had been driven from their homes, and three hundred thousand had starved to death.

The United Nations had commissioned us, along with troops from several other nations, to take care of this bully once and for all, ushering him toward a trial for crimes against humanity. In the two months Task Force Ranger had been in Mogadishu, we'd already conducted six raids into the dusty, chaotic city, nabbing key players in Aidid's militia each time. Cooperative Somalis who wanted a better life for their country fed us tips on where to look. Soon our small helicopters swooped down from the sky to drop special operators on the designated rooftop or in alleys nearby. They kicked in the doors, immediately threw flash-bang grenades to stun everyone inside, and then handcuffed them with flexbands before the targets knew what hit them.

Meanwhile, Rangers were already arriving on the larger Black Hawk helicopters, which hovered thirty feet or so over each of the four corners of the block. Three-inch ropes were flung downward, and Rangers slid down to the street like firefighters descending a station pole—a maneuver called "fast-roping." The instant the Rangers hit the ground, they took control of the intersection, thereby setting up a controlled perimeter that no one could penetrate.

This rectangle stayed in place until a column of vehicles rolled up to the door of the target building to load up the captured. Normally this was my mission to lead. The Rangers at the four corners, on receiving a radio signal, collapsed back in our direction to jump on the convoy themselves, along with the special operators. We raced out of the neighborhood before most people even had a clue what was going down.

Two for the Price of One

On the afternoon of October 3, 1993, we received word that a high-level meeting was under way at a certain three-story building on Hawlwadig Road, just a block north of the Olympic Hotel. Sunday was a normal business day in this Muslim country; their day of worship is Friday. At this meeting, not one but *two* of the big shots were supposedly present: Omar Salad, Aidid's top political adviser, and Abdi "Qeybdid" Hassan Awale, his interior minister. What a lucky break!

Yes, it would have been nicer not to have to go in during the late afternoon, when crowds of people were around and paying attention. We'd rather have done this raid during the night or early morning, of course. But the opportunity for a two-fer was too good to pass up.

"Struecker, you know how to find this place?" Lieutenant Colonel Danny McKnight asked as we stood in the JOC (Joint Operations Center). By studying satellite maps, I had become something of an expert in the geography of the city. It was a challenge, since no street signs existed, and you definitely weren't going to get help from MapQuest or AAA. But gradually I had built up my memory bank of local landmarks and what streets led where.

"Yes, sir," I replied. "I've driven by there several times. It's just a few blocks east of the Bakara Market, which is not the most pleasant neighborhood for us, as you know. But we can definitely get there." This was the heart of Aidid territory, where open-air booths sold everything from cucumbers to rugs to rifles.

"Okay. We're moving out in ten minutes. Birds lift off first, and you'll be heading up the road almost immediately after." That was the way it usually ran for Ranger missions; we had to be ready to go on very short notice.

While the helicopters were loading up, I lined up the ground column at the gate. My Humvee (army-talk for HMMWV, High Mobility Multi-Wheeled Vehicle—in other words, the prototype for what eventually became the Hummer in today's auto marketplace) would lead the way, with young Private First Class Jeremy Kerr as my driver. He was getting all kinds of new experience here in Somalia— first time to drive a military vehicle, first time to wear night goggles. Everything was a steep learning curve for Jeremy.

In the back, behind a metal bomb protection plate, was Sergeant Dominick Pilla, the best machine gunner I'd ever seen. He was a big, funny guy from "New Joyzee," whose practical jokes and skits kept the entire battalion entertained. Beside him was young Specialist Tim Moynihan, a bongo-playing guy with thick black hair who could have grown a great-looking beard had regulations allowed. He was well-liked and popular among all the guys.

Up on top in the turret was Private First Class Brad Paulson manning the big .50 caliber machine gun. He was a small-sized fellow from the Midwest who almost looked young enough to still be in high school, except for his "high-and-tight" military haircut. I thought of him as a kid brother.

Right behind our vehicle was the other half of our squad in a second Humvee, led by my right hand, Sergeant Danny Mitchell. His super-slow Arkansas drawl made some people assume he wasn't the sharpest knife in the drawer, which, in fact, was opposite of the truth. I soon realized he was qualified to fill in for me at any time. We'd worked together a long time and could almost read each other's minds. He was incredibly loyal and would do anything I asked.

Next came more Humvees and three five-ton flatbed trucks for holding lots of people—a total of twelve vehicles in all. I was the lead navigator, while Lieutenant Colonel McKnight, farther back in a Humvee, would be calling the main plays.

We roared out of the gate as soon as the signal came that the helicopters, already in the air, were about to launch their assault. The distance to cover was no more than a four-minute drive into the sandy, garbage-littered streets of Mogadishu. We dodged burned-out vehicles along the way and swerved around piles of loose tires, old furniture, and wood scraps that residents had set on fire to draw attention to previous gun battles. I found it odd that instead of running away from trouble, the residents almost seemed magnetized by it, coming out of their crumbling houses to get in on the action.

As we got close to the hotel, I instructed Jeremy Kerr to turn right. Actually, I spoke a block or two too soon. It was the only wrong turn I took during my whole time in Somalia. The confusion was quickly remedied, however, and the whole convoy reassembled behind the hotel—a five-story white building with lots of balconies—to await our next move.

We heard shots in the distance; it was clear that the Rangers at the four corners were taking fire from Aidid's hidden militia. They weren't about to let us capture their leaders unchallenged. Battered pickup trucks with their backs full of rifle-waving militia began screeching around corners.

But at the target house, things were progressing smoothly. The time for extraction of the bad guys was almost here. The main point of this mission—getting the two men—was nearly wrapped up.

JUST A MINUTE . . .

Then came the fateful moment when I first heard about a "small problem": "Hey, Struecker, we've got a casualty," came Danny McKnight's voice through the radio. "You need to go get him, put him on your vehicle, and take him back to base."

I got out and walked back to his Humvee. "Sir, what's up?" I asked. "What's going on?"

"I don't know who it is, but his condition doesn't sound too good. You need to get him out of here. I'll give you one of the cargo Humvees [the military version of a pickup truck], and your two with your squad can escort him back to the airfield."

"Who are we talking about, sir? And where is he?"

"I don't know the name, but he's one of the guys in Sergeant Eversmann's chalk just up ahead. You can ask Captain Steele if you want—he's right by the target building."

Steele was our overall Ranger company commander, a big man who had played football at the University of Georgia. I walked in his direction. The closer I got, the more the hostile fire seemed to increase. The Somalis weren't hitting much of anything, as usual, but they were definitely turning up the volume. I had been shot at before, enough to tell by the sound when the rounds were getting close. I crouched near a wall while I talked with Captain Steele to get a better fix on where to go.

The problem was this: as Eversmann's men had fast-roped down from their Black Hawk helicopter to secure the northwest corner of the perimeter, a young Ranger named Todd Blackburn had missed the rope as he jumped out. Either that, or he took a bullet into his bulletproof vest, which didn't penetrate but successfully stunned him right at the point of grabbing the rope. To make matters worse, the Black Hawk was higher than normal from the ground, due to some power lines on that corner (not that Mogadishu's electricity supply was even functioning anymore). Todd Blackburn had plunged some seventy feet and hit the street headfirst with a sickening thud.

I ran back to the convoy, grabbed a stretcher off the back of the cargo vehicle, and hollered for Moynihan to follow me. When we got to Eversmann's corner, I saw a medic working furiously on the guy in the street, trying to get his airway open. I moved to catch a glimpse of Blackburn's face, and it was not a pretty sight. Blood was coming from his nose, his mouth, and one of his ears. His eyes were rolled back into his head.

He still had his helmet on; nobody wanted to remove it for fear of jarring him. *He's hurt his back,* I thought. *We're going to have to be really careful moving him.*

We gingerly lifted Blackburn onto the stretcher, then hoisted it up and started back down the street. As we ran the enemy fire grew worse, to the point that we had to take shelter for a moment. *Man, these guys are coming from about every window and rooftop, aren't they?* I thought. I had hoped we could get this job done without rousing the whole militia.

In spite of the hammering, we fought our way back to the vehicles, where we loaded Blackburn on the back of the cargo Humvee. A medic quickly went to work on him, totally exposed to the incoming fire. A special operator jumped aboard to fire back and try to protect the medic and Todd.

After a quick consultation with Lieutenant Colonel McKnight to tell him I was leaving now with three vehicles, and to advise him on how the rest could find their way home without my map, we moved out. Turning right at the first corner, we headed for the next street to make another right back toward the ocean and out of the city. "We need to take it slow, so we don't break Blackburn's neck," I instructed my guys. "Dodge every pothole you can."

At the second corner, however, it was as if the whole city opened up on us. As we threaded our way through the narrow street with two- and three-story buildings on both sides, bullets were flying our way from every direction. We fought back with everything we had: our personal M-16s, submachine guns, Paulson's .50 cal up on top. It was definitely intense.

Paulson was swinging back and forth, shooting all over. "Paulson, just take the left side!" I hollered. "Pilla, you cover the right!" I concentrated on fighting the danger ahead of us.

We had stormed our way through about five blocks when we reached National Street, a four-lane boulevard. A right turn here would head us out of the slums and back toward the base. We were just rounding the corner when Dom Pilla spotted a gunman leveling his AK-47 right at him. Dom fired at the guy—who in the very same instant fired at Dom's head. The two shots were virtually simultaneous. The next thing I knew, Moynihan was screaming in the back: "Pilla's hit! He's shot in the head!"

I whirled to look around the corner of the metal plate. Dom Pilla had slumped over into Tim Moynihan's lap—and there was blood everywhere. The whole back of the Humvee was bright red. I couldn't believe how much of an effect one bullet could have.

It had, in fact, entered just above Dom's left eye and proceeded to blow out the whole back of his head. Just an inch higher, and it would have clanged off Dom's helmet. But it had struck flesh and brain instead.

"What do we do? Dom's killed!" Moynihan yelled. At this my other two guys, Kerr and Paulson up on top, began freaking out as well. For a second I panicked on the inside. I had just lost a very good soldier, a man I was responsible for—and a good friend. I swallowed hard. This operation was going seriously askew.

THE GAUNTLET

I couldn't let myself think more about all that. I had to detach myself and jump back into tactical mode. Otherwise a horrible situation would get even worse. *Take charge, Jeff,* I told myself.

"Moynihan," I said in a steady voice, "stop what you're doing. Take your weapon and face right; pick up Dominick's sector of fire." He quieted down as he followed my order.

"Kerr, step on it!" I said to the driver. "Fly down this road as fast as you can." No more worrying about jostling Todd Blackburn's neck or back in the vehicle behind us. Better that than any more of us getting killed in this maelstrom of hot lead. We couldn't afford to poke along as fat, easy targets in the middle of a hostile city.

We roared down National Street for a good mile until we approached the big food distribution center. Twice a day in Mogadishu,

UNICEF, CARE, Food for the Hungry, and other agencies handed out relief, and every starving Somali showed up to get their next meal. Wouldn't you know—this just happened to be the hour of the evening handout. The road was packed with literally thousands of people. I couldn't even see to the far side of the crowd. Meanwhile, we were still getting hammered from the buildings on both sides.

"Paulson!" I hollered up to my gunner. "We've got to clear a path. Start shooting over their heads. Don't kill anybody, but make them think you're shooting at them, so they'll scatter." To help get the crowd's attention, I threw half a dozen nonlethal grenades.

The sea of humanity at the distribution center started to part— slowly. "Hurry up, people!" my driver yelled. The hail of bullets continued.

Finally, I couldn't stall any longer. "Just floor it," I told Kerr. "They'll get out of the way." We plunged toward the crowd and eventually reached the far side of it.

On our way again and building speed, the hostile fire slacked off a bit. Instead of getting shot at from fifty places at once, it was down to five places at once. Just then the voice of Platoon Sergeant Bob Gallagher, my direct superior on this particular mission, came on the radio. "How are things goin'?"

I definitely did not want to answer that. Most of our unit had heard about Blackburn's fall by now, but almost nobody knew about Pilla. And bad news has a way of messing with soldiers' minds— even highly trained Rangers. I ignored the question.

Gallagher's voice came again. "How's it goin', Struecker?"

I couldn't stiff-arm him again. Finally I said, "I don't want to talk about it."

That reply, of course, only piqued his interest.

"You got any casualties?"

"Yeah, one." *Just let it go, man!* my mind was begging.

"Who is he, and what's his status?"

I took a deep breath. "It's Pilla," I finally answered.

"What's his status?"

Another breath. I was cornered; I had to answer the question.

"He's dead."

The radio, which had been crackling with lots of conversation all across the city between our various units, suddenly went quiet. Nobody said another word. Soldiers were simply stunned. This was the first man we'd lost since landing in Somalia. The invincible Ranger Regiment had been nicked by an untrained, impoverished Somali gunman with little more than a grudge to pursue.

I switched frequency on the radio and called the JOC back at the base. "Hey, I'm about two minutes out. Get the surgeons ready for us, okay? I've got one guy who got hurt on the fast rope, and another guy just got hit in the head—he may not have survived." I was pretty sure he hadn't, but then, I didn't know for certain.

We were making good progress until we came upon a Toyota pickup truck doing no more than ten miles an hour. Somalis were hanging all over it, the way you often see in poor countries; some were just barely grasping a piece of metal to gain a footing.

"Lay on the horn!" I yelled at my driver. He did so—with no response. The truck just kept poking along.

We were still getting shot at from shadowy silhouettes. "Okay, run him off the road!" I ordered Kerr. "We gotta get our guy back to a doctor before anybody else gets blasted."

Kerr looked at me as if I were crazy, but then proceeded to move up and bump the back end of the Toyota. The truck swerved, banged into something on the side of the road, and swung back into the lane again.

"Hit him again!" Kerr came up behind the truck, made contact, and kept pushing this time until the lane was finally cleared.

Soon after, we whipped through the gate into the airport compound, where a scene of frenzy confronted us. Guys were running everywhere, loading helicopters, loading vehicles, scrambling for more ammo. The medical team was waiting as I had requested. They began pulling Pilla out of the back of my Humvee. When I saw his face as white as a snow-bank, I didn't have to wonder anymore.

"Just leave him alone," I said to Doc Marsh. "He's gone. Go to the other vehicle. Blackburn's over there." Medics began racing in that direction.

INTERMISSION

There was nothing more for me to do. I walked away from my vehicle as a wave of fury swept over me. It had been the worst, most intense forty minutes of my life. What a stupid situation. The mission had been going so well—until this. We had lost one of the best guys ever to wear the Ranger scroll on his uniform, and another one was in serious jeopardy. This whole thing was disgusting.

I took off my helmet in frustration and whipped it like a Frisbee across the airfield. It bounced along and clattered to a stop against a stack of sandbags. I wanted to scream in anger. This was so, so wrong.

God, like, so what's the deal here? I vented. *How come this all fell apart on me? What am I supposed to do next?*

I received my answer to the last question when I turned around and looked into the faces of my squad. Their eyes were huge. They had never seen me, their leader, show emotion. Had I lost my grip?

I picked up my helmet and placed it under my arm as I walked back in their direction. Doctors and medics were still running back and forth. One came around the corner with a wooden backboard for transporting Todd Blackburn. I moved past them to face my men again.

An awkward moment passed. I realized they were waiting for me to speak. I searched for words to explain all the bullets and blood we'd just been through. I tried to think of how I could smooth over the hurt they were feeling. But I couldn't come up with anything. So I kept my mouth shut.

Just then the air was changed by the approach of Lieutenant Larry Moores, the officer in charge of my platoon. A man well into his thirties, he was older than most lieutenants and was known to be a meticulous planner. Yet he trusted us subordinates greatly, having been in our shoes as an enlisted man before he was commissioned. His face was drained; I knew immediately that something was very wrong.

"What's up, sir?" I asked.

Very slowly he answered, "Another Black Hawk has gone down. You need to get your squad ready to go back in. We need to get to the crash site."

"What do you mean, *another?*" I cried. "We're losing birds now?"

"Yes. Wolcott's went down while you were out, and now we just found out that Mike Durant's is down as well."

I was dumbfounded. *Oh, God, no,* I thought as he walked away. After all the disaster we'd just come through, we were being told to head right back into it again?

"Acknowledging the fact that a Ranger is a more elite soldier who arrives at the cutting edge of battle by land, sea, or air . . ." That's what our creed says. "Readily will I display the intestinal fortitude required to fight on to the Ranger objective and complete the mission." Now was the time to prove it.

"Sergeant Mitchell!" I called to my team leader. "Get your vehicle down to the supply point and get more ammo! Get some for us, too, while you're at it. And don't forget to fuel up.

"Moynihan! Thomas! Go get some water, and make sure there's nothing in the vehicles that's not absolutely mission-essential! Get some night-vision goggles, too. This might take awhile." They stared at me for just a moment and then did as they had been told.

DEATH UP CLOSE

I was just about to pass out more orders to the remaining squad members when Sergeant John Macejunas, one of the special operators, walked over. A former Ranger with blond hair and a deep tan, he was the epitome of fitness. Knowing what I'd been told to do, he offered a bit of free advice.

"Sergeant, you don't want to take your men back out in all that blood. You need to clean up your vehicle first."

I turned to look at the mess in the back of my Humvee. He was right. If we headed back into battle with Pilla's blood splattered all over the place, it would definitely psych out my guys. I should have realized that on my own.

"Roger that," I replied to Macejunas.

I looked at Kerr and Paulson, the last two guys without a job to do. Neither of them was more than about nineteen years old. I could see in their eyes that they were already overwhelmed. How could I order them to clean up the blood of a man they so respected? I should do this myself. I'd already carted away several body bags in my military life. I'd had my hands in blood more than once. If I asked some young guy to do this, would I be ruining him for life?

Finally I said, "Men, I could use some help cleaning up this vehicle—but I'm not going to make you do it. If you want to volunteer, okay. But if you'd rather not, I understand. Just go help load up more fuel and ammo instead."

The two privates first class didn't walk away. They stayed with me as we pulled the Humvee over to the tanker, parking it to slope downhill so water would drain out the back of it. Mogadishu had no running water; this would strictly be a bucket operation. We got a big sponge, a little yellow brush, and started sloshing water over the metal.

It was an awful mess. We scrubbed away for probably five minutes. I looked at my hands and saw the scratches from thrusting the barrel of my rifle out the Humvee window. I knew I should probably be wearing surgical gloves, but I didn't want to bother running to the other side of the hangar to get some. So I just plunged my hands into the gore and tried not to think about it. We doused the vehicle with bucket after bucket of water, until finally the grim evidence of death sank away into the desert sand.

I picked up the ammo can that Pilla had been using. It was perhaps two-thirds full of his blood, with unused bullets swimming in it. *Man, we're gonna need this*, I told myself as I ran the belt of ammunition through a bucket of clean water. We'd probably be using every bullet we could gather.

As we worked, the radio in front kept transmitting the sounds of the worsening battle in the city. It seemed that dozens of voices were talking on top of each other—and what struck me was not just the fact of guys getting pinned down and shot at, but even more, the rising urgency in their tone. Everybody sounded like he was yelling at somebody a thousand miles away. Calls for medevacs, pleas for reinforcement—you could sense the wave of fear starting to sweep across the battlefield. The situation was growing worse by the minute.

I hung on every word. With each new voice, I pictured in my mind the face of the speaker. It was becoming clear that we weren't just battling a thousand or so militia fighters in the streets of Mogadishu; we could have handled that many. This was sounding more like ten thousand. There seemed to be no end to their resources.

Occasionally my heart would soar as a commander gave confident directions to his soldiers on the radio. Then just as soon, my spirit would sink as another frazzled sergeant said, "We're getting clobbered here; we really need some help." I knew the sensation all too well.

Finally I said to Kerr, "Turn the radio off. I don't even want to hear what's happening for a while." We didn't have time to be distracted anyway; we needed to get ready to move out again.

The relative silence allowed new thoughts to surface in my mind. *I'm going to die tonight. And what's just as bad, I'm going to get every one of my men killed. I just know it. There's no way we can survive another run back into that city. Tomorrow this squad is going to have ten dead Rangers instead of just one.*

My mind wandered to my wife, Dawn, newly pregnant. *My child is never going to know his daddy,* I thought. *This is it, tonight. How is she going to manage having a baby and raising it all by herself?*

I started to pray. It was a very simple prayer. *God, I'm in deep trouble, as you can see. I need help. I'm not saying you should get me out of this. I just need your help.*

Still scrubbing away at the blood, my attention veered off somehow to an ancient scene: Jesus praying in the Garden of Gethsemane. I was no longer in Somalia at that moment. I was echoing the prayer of Jesus: "My Father! If it is possible, let this cup of suffering be taken away from me. Yet I want your will, not mine" (Matthew 26:39).

My life was in God's hands, I told myself, and the only thing I could do at this critical point was to trust him with the course of events. The hour and circumstances of my death were up to him. I could definitely die tonight. Of course, I could get killed crossing the street back in America, too. I could slip on a bar of soap in the shower and hit my head.

If I survived this night, I eventually would get to go home to Dawn and our new baby. If I died, I'd go home to be with Jesus in heaven. Either way, I'd be a winner. So maybe I needed to stop being afraid of the upcoming battle after all.

A second realization then came my way. I had a leadership role to fulfill. *God, please don't let me do anything stupid that puts the rest of my men into a slaughter tonight,* I prayed. *If any of them get killed, I sure don't want it to be my fault.*

The sense of peace I felt was almost surreal. I snapped back out of my reverie, took a visual inspection of the vehicle, and said, "Men, we're good. Let's load up and get ready to move." We returned to the rest of the squad, where Danny Mitchell had the preparations in good order.

I could tell that one of my slightly older men, Brad Thomas, was definitely struggling. He had been married just a few months before coming here. Now I was asking him to head straight back into the teeth of destruction. He pulled me aside to say, "Sergeant, you know I *really* don't want to go back out."

This was a costly thing for a Ranger to say. He knew there would be consequences for shrinking from the fight. He had apparently weighed that price and decided to pay it.

Now what was I, his sergeant, going to do? I reviewed the options in my mind. *I could end his career in the Ranger Regiment right here by saying, "Go back to your cot and pack up your stuff—you're on the next plane out of here!"*

I opted instead for a more nuanced approach. "Listen, I understand how you feel," I said in a low tone. "I'm married, too. Don't think of yourself as a coward. I know you're scared. I've never been in a situation quite like this, either. But we've got to go. It's our job. The difference between being a coward and a hero is not whether you're scared or not. It's what you do while you're scared."

I don't know to this day where I got that line. It was nothing I had read in a book or heard from a speaker. I guess God just gave it to me when I needed it. I turned my attention back to the demands of the moment.

Brad Thomas walked away momentarily, thinking hard. I climbed into my Humvee and in a minute glanced at the rearview mirror. There I saw Brad climbing aboard with the rest of us. We were ready to roll in search of the downed Black Hawk that needed us.

The base of a flagpole where the U.S. flag flies over an undisclosed location in the Global War on Terrorism.

Two

QUESTIONS IN THE NIGHT

THAT DAY IN SOMALIA WAS NOT THE FIRST TIME I HAD BEEN genuinely spooked about dying. Long before, as a little kid growing up in Fort Dodge, Iowa, I was strangely drawn to the mystery of death. I would lie awake in bed at night wondering: *When am I going to die? How is it going to happen? What will it be like two seconds afterward?*

Nothing in my home situation triggered this, so far as I can remember. We didn't talk about death any more than the average family. I don't remember being taken to a funeral or a cemetery. Nobody read scary stories to me as a boy. No grandparents had passed away at that point.

My dad was a quiet, unemotional man who held down a steady job as a postal worker. My mother was a hard worker as well, dedicated to taking care of us four kids. Angie was four years older than I; Troy was three years older. I was third in the birth order, with Jenny coming along two years after I was born. We lived a normal life in a town of twenty-five thousand people in the middle of the Corn Belt.

We weren't a picture-perfect household, however; my parents divorced when I was four or five years old. We kids were definitely rocked by this, and when given the choice of which parent to live with, I didn't know what to say. Angie and Jenny were going to stay with Mom; Troy was going to live with Dad. What should I do? I didn't have much of a relationship with my father, so I opted to stick with the girls and Mom, who found employment as a bill collector.

I had just finished first grade when the nightmares began.

I'm climbing on the playground equipment at school. All the kids are running and yelling and having a great time. My friends and I are racing to the top of the jungle gym. I scramble with all my might and get there first. I am the champion!

Next we move to the circular slide. It's very slick. Instead of climbing the ladder and sliding down from the top, we challenge each other to climb up from the bottom. Who can get to the top before all the others?

I jump into the competition—but wait! What's this? I'm climbing up the outside of the circular apparatus. Nobody has attempted this before. I'm dangling over nothing but air as I ascend the slide.

I'm aware of the danger. But I have to prove my courage. I complete the first turn and press on toward the second. The ground is receding farther and farther beneath me. I'm getting a little dizzy looking down. If I fall, I'll be in big trouble.

I complete the second turn and push still upward. Only half a turn left to reach my pedestal of fame. I'm within inches of the top. I can already taste my victory. I stretch for the metal railing on the top landing—where is it? I can't feel it.

My arms begin to flail uncontrollably. The landing whooshes away in my vision as I plunge into the void. The ground is starting to come up fast now. Kids are scattering in all directions. I'm going to slam into the gravel!

The bed shudders beneath me. I jerk onto my side as a taste of nausea rises in my mouth. My stomach heaves with a sinking feeling. I'm not fully awake, but even in my half-conscious state I'm terrified. I fall back to sleep.

Now I'm whisked away to the middle of Interstate 35. It's late on a foggy night. Drivers are picking their way through the soup at reduced speed but still trying to reach their destinations without too much delay.

I'm trying to get up and run across the highway. It's very wide, and my legs are too heavy. I chug onto the asphalt. The lights of an oncoming car are breaking through the fog. They're getting closer. Can the driver see me here? Probably not.

The noise intensifies. It's not a car—it's a diesel truck. He's going to hit me in less than a second. There's no hope to get out of his way. I can't move fast enough. I raise my arms in a feeble attempt to protect my face—

Once again I am startled away from my doom. I toss and try to catch my breath. Why do I dream these kinds of things almost every night? I'm so scared.

My bed transforms itself into a coffin. I'm lying inside. All is quiet. Then I hear the sound of the mechanical crank turning. The straps underneath are being lengthened to slowly lower me into the hole. Miraculously I see through the lid as the men turn the handle.

The coffin settles onto the bottom, and the turning stops. The men pull the sturdy straps out from under me. They pack up their hoist and then turn to get their shovels.

The first load of dirt is dropped into the grave. Then come the second, the third, and the fourth. The pace increases with each shovelful. The dirt rises on all sides, sealing me into the ground. Eventually the lid is covered as well. All is now totally dark.

I'm still thinking with full clarity, even though I've been entombed. *What happens next?* I wonder. *Is there anything more out there after death? Will I just lie here and get cold when winter comes? I think I'm going to throw up—*

More than a few times, at two or three in the morning, I would get out of bed and go seeking for answers to my tormenting questions. My mother was usually away, working a second job. I wished she were home; this night shift was killing her. But in her absence, I awakened my older sister—again.

"Angie—Angie," I whispered as I knelt beside her bed, touching her shoulder.

A low grunt came through the darkness.

"Are you awake? Can I talk to you?"

"It's late," she mumbled. "What do you want?"

"I have to ask you a question."

"What is it?" she asked in a sleepy voice.

"Where do people go when they die?" I said, lowering myself to the floor.

Angie opened her eyes and looked at me. "We already talked about that last time, and the time before that," she replied with a touch of irritation. "They go to heaven."

"How do they get there?"

"God brings them there, I guess."

This was never enough to satisfy me. "Angie, what's heaven like?" I persisted.

She paused. Then she said, "It's where you get to do anything you want to do. You get to eat anything you want to eat. It's always warm and sunny. And everybody is always happy."

Then came my crucial question: "Does everybody get to go to heaven?"

"Of course," she told me. "Now go back to bed. Just think happy thoughts about flowers and bunny rabbits and stuff like that, okay? Get some sleep."

I cautiously retreated to my bed. *Everyone goes to heaven, she had said. Maybe I can make it to morning without more nightmares.*

VAGABONDS

This pattern persisted through my grade school years. I developed a reputation in the family as the kid who was always worrying about death. In the daytime I was not bothered, but when night fell, the familiar fears would pounce. Angie grew weary of trying to comfort me.

My mother was occupied with issues of her own. When she found a job that paid just a bit more than she was currently earning, she made the shift, regardless of location. She filled in with second jobs, such as waitressing, when she could. For a while she was even an over-the-road truck driver, which meant we kids had a string of live-in nannies, none of whom lasted very long.

During my growing-up years, Mom married and divorced three more times. A stepfather would show up in our house for a while and then be on his way within a couple of years. I never built much of a connection with any of the three; they weren't around long enough.

It seemed that our household was in perpetual upheaval, due to frequent moves. By the time I finished high school, I had lived in five different states and some twenty different houses. I attended four different high schools—three of them in the first two years.

To relocate in the middle of a school year was especially tough. I well remember the feeling of being the new kid when everybody else's friendships were already in place. I got to the point of not trying to build relationships with other kids because I knew we'd be on the road before long anyway. I ate lunch by myself and stayed in the shadows.

I did venture out on Sunday mornings, however, to walk to a nearby church. I don't know why—nobody else would go with me. My father had always said he was Lutheran—standard practice for just about anybody in northern Iowa with a German name. But I don't remember him attending church very much, or anyone else in my family. As a growing boy, I just walked to whatever was close.

"Mom, can I have a dollar?" I'd ask before heading out the door. She probably thought I wanted to buy a candy bar or a Coke. But what I wanted was something to put in the offering plate at church. I didn't want people staring at me and thinking I was poor.

As a result of this input, I was a fairly moral boy growing up; I didn't get in trouble. But I can't say I had any relationship or closeness to God. Church was just something I thought I should be doing.

When I was thirteen years old, we moved to Gallatin, Tennessee, right outside of Nashville. I started walking to a nearby church called Hendersonville Chapel. A young couple in their early twenties who attended there lived in the apartment next to us.

One night around eight o'clock, they came over to see me. Mom was at work, as usual. Angie, seventeen by now, lived with our grandparents in Iowa.

"Hey, Jeff, can we come in and talk to you?" they asked.

"Sure. Have a seat," I said.

They seemed a little nervous. First one, then the other, would stare down at their feet. *What's going on?* I wondered.

"We just thought it would be a good idea to share with you about how to be right with God," the guy started. "You know, the truth is that we're all sinners—you, me, all of us."

I had no problem with that. I clearly understood that I wasn't perfect.

"But God is willing to forgive our sins. That's why he sent Jesus Christ to this earth. Jesus died on the cross to pay for all our sins. We just have to ask him—"

"Well, wait a minute," I objected. "Who says there's really a God up there anyway?" I began to derail the conversation with questions about evolution—I'd had some science classes in school. I brought up other difficulties I could muster. "I know the minister talks about God every Sunday," I said, "but he's never proved that it's true."

The couple was gracious enough to listen to me. They didn't try to argue me down. They answered what questions they could, and frankly admitted the ones they didn't know.

On the matter of the existence of God, they raised the evidence of creation. Where did everything in the universe come from? "Science can take you back to early material—the egg before the chicken, the pine cone before the pine tree—but where did *those* things come from? If you go back far enough, you have to admit that in the real beginning, something came from nothing. Hence, there must be a God who started it all."

This discussion went on for twenty minutes or so. I began to track with what they were saying. I could tell these people were genuinely concerned for me.

Jenny, my younger sister, was off in her room doing something at the time. I inserted, "Hey, do you guys want to talk to Jenny, too?"

"Well, not right now," they answered. "You're the one we know from seeing you at church. We came over mainly to talk to you."

They clearly explained my need for a Savior. They told how to confess my sin and receive Christ into my life.

"Well, my big sister always said that everybody goes to heaven," I said. "Are you saying something different?"

"We're just saying what the Bible says," the woman responded. "It says that God is more than happy to welcome those into heaven who have accepted the gift of salvation."

"When you sincerely turn your heart over to Christ," they said, "he will make a difference in your life. You'll know it right away, in fact. Think about what we've told you and then take the step if you want."

They didn't push me to do so right on the spot. They left that evening with the ball in my court.

Peace on the Inside

That night before crawling into bed, I knelt at the side and recited the prayer they had outlined. Then I went to sleep. The next morning, I frankly couldn't tell anything "different" about my life. I went through my normal day.

The next night at bedtime, I thought, *Well, maybe I didn't say the prayer right. Maybe I should do it again.* So I knelt down for the second time and went through the prayer. The next morning, however, I again sensed no change.

I kept this up for about two weeks. I got to the point of telling myself this was a bunch of nonsense. It might be good for my neighbors, but it sure wasn't working for me. Maybe it was all a hoax.

Then, lying in bed once again, I remembered what they had said: "This has to be a sincere decision. You have to mean it with your whole heart." I realized I hadn't done that. I'd just been mouthing the words.

That night to the best of my ability I prayed again, using my own words this time. I didn't recite the standard prayer I'd heard. I told the Lord I was sincerely sorry for my sin and wanted to be forgiven. I wanted to be part of God's family.

And then I added something uniquely important to me: "God, I don't want to go to hell. I don't want to be afraid of death anymore like I've been my whole life. I want to know that I'm going to heaven."

That night I turned out the light and closed my eyes—a thirteen-year-old kid in a single mom's apartment—and slept peacefully. The dreams about dying and death never returned, even as the years went by.

I realize some may find my story too simple. "One little prayer, and your seven-year obsession with death just vanished? Yeah, right." Well, all I can say is, that's truly what happened. I was there, and I was greatly relieved.

What I needed at this point in my life was peace. My neighbors hadn't actually used that word when they talked to me; instead, they spoke of sin and the need for a Savior. But when I received Christ into my life, the real change was the arrival of peace on the inside. That's what I had been craving. I'd never had it before, and a new day had dawned.

A field worship service in Louisiana with paratroopers from the 82nd Airborne Division.

Three

INTO THE UNKNOWN

BY MY SENIOR YEAR OF HIGH SCHOOL, WE HAD WANDERED back to Fort Dodge, Iowa, and I was facing what to do with the rest of my life. I had no strong sense of purpose, no shining goal to reach for. Though I kept going to church, we had moved so often that I hadn't received a lot of follow-up instruction on my life as a Christian or on how to make important decisions. I was just doing the teenage-guy thing, going to school, fixing up my cherished blue '71 Mustang sports coupe, and working at Burger King.

I definitely paid attention when two good-looking, dark-haired sophomores—twins—came to work there. They went to Catholic school, so I hadn't met them on campus. The one named Dawn and I soon became good friends at work and started dating. I wanted to impress her (as well as the boss) with my work ethic, and was promoted to assistant manager.

One day in the spring of 1987, just a few months before graduation, the district manager stopped by to talk to me. "I hear really good things about you," she said with a smile. "What are you going to do after high school? As a matter of fact, I'll soon have an opening in the Burger King up in Spencer. If you want to go up there and manage that one, I'd definitely hire you." (Spencer is a smaller town about ninety miles northwest of Fort Dodge.)

It was a remarkable opportunity for an eighteen-year-old boy. I didn't consider myself to be college material—that was for sure. My grades weren't going to open any doors for me. So I said to the manager, "I'll think about it. I'll let you know."

Her question jarred me. Was this going to be my career—running a fast-food joint? Nothing wrong with that, of course—but five or ten years down the road, after I married and had kids, did I want them going to school saying, "Guess what my daddy does? He makes hamburgers"?

The next week at school, I said to a friend of mine named Tony, "So what are you going to do after you graduate?"

He was ready with an immediate answer. "Join the army."

"Really?"

"Yep. I've already signed up."

"How come?"

"Well, my dad was a Navy SEAL back in Vietnam. He's told me a lot about opportunities in the military. So I'm going for it. You ought to come see the army recruiter with me; he's a cool guy named Mike Walker, and you can find out all kinds of stuff."

The only military history in my family that I knew of was my maternal grandfather, who had been a tank commander in World War II, serving in North Africa. His daughter—my mom—was the total opposite. A child of the 1960s, she did not have the slightest tolerance for anything to do with war. Nobody else had served in the armed forces.

I guessed it wouldn't hurt to get some information. So Tony and I went by the recruiting office. We sat down, my friend introduced me, and Mr. Walker said, "So, son, what would you like to know?"

"Uh, I don't know," I stammered. We made small talk for a few minutes, and I finally framed an intelligent question. "What's the toughest job in the army? What's the absolutely hardest thing you can do?"

A second recruiter sitting at the next desk jumped in at that moment. "Special Forces," he announced with assurance.

"No, it's not," Mike Walker retorted. "It's Airborne Rangers."

I didn't know much about either one, so I just sat listening as the two of them argued about which was more demanding. Finally Mr. Walker turned to me and said, "Look, here's an example to explain the difference. If I line up five Rangers at the base of the Gateway Arch in St. Louis, and I also bring five Special Forces Green Berets, and I tell 'em all to get to the top of the arch, here's what'll happen. The Rangers will take a grappling hook on the end of a knotted hand rope, heave it up over the top of the arch, and climb hand-over-hand to the summit. Meanwhile, the Green Berets will go inside to the tourist shop, push the elevator button, and ride to the top so they can be waiting there when the Rangers arrive."

I'm sure some readers who are current or former Green Berets will take offense at that comparison. But as a high-school kid, I bought it all the way. The man continued, "If you're really interested in being a Ranger, take this video home and watch it. It's a feature that 20/20 did on Ranger School awhile back. You'll get a very good idea from this."

That night when Mom wasn't around, I popped in the video. I was riveted by what I saw. These were the toughest, most daring, best-trained men I'd ever seen. They excelled in quick-strike, highly disciplined combat in all kinds of conditions—hence the red lightning bolt across the middle of the Ranger crest.

I learned that to be a Ranger you have to get through intense training that stretches you to the ultimate limit. Ranger School was fifty-eight straight days of blood, guts, and exhaustion. Thousands of guys dropped out along the way—they weren't tough enough. If you saw a guy with a Ranger patch, called a "tab," on his left shoulder, you knew you were looking at the best of the best.

I went back to the recruiting station the next afternoon after school, video in hand. "Where do I sign up?" I asked Mr. Walker. "That's what I want to be—a Ranger." This was the road to discovering my limits. *Did I have what it would take? Could I handle the challenge?* I wanted to know. There was no financial incentive; Rangers didn't earn a dime more than any other soldier of equal rank. It was all about being the best.

Sure, it would be dangerous. But so what? I'd probably be staring death straight in the face sometimes. My faith since age thirteen had overcome the fear of dying, I thought—but let's find out for sure. I would never know without going for the hardest test imaginable. Plus, my rather jumbled and disorganized home life, with all the moves we'd made, could use some structure.

Mr. Walker nodded. "Okay, the first thing you do is go through thirteen weeks of basic training for the infantry. In your case, that'll happen at Fort Benning, Georgia." He began outlining the procedures I had to follow and brought out the forms I needed to sign.

I found out I couldn't directly get a guaranteed army Ranger contract at the beginning. Instead, the recruiter said I should go to Airborne School right after basic training. "That's another three weeks. And sometime during that process, two Rangers in black berets are going to stop by and ask who wants to join them. That's when you put up your hand. If you do, they'll at least give you a shot. From there on, it's up to you to see if you can make it."

FIRST CHALLENGES

I was pumped when I arrived home that evening. "Guess what, Mom," I announced, "I've finally figured out what I'm going to do after high school. I'm going to become a Ranger!"

She looked at me blankly. "You mean, like a forest ranger with one of those Smokey-the-Bear hats?"

"No! An *army* Ranger. They're the elite of all the soldiers. They get to do the coolest stuff."

"You *what?*" she screeched. "You're going to be one of those paid killers in the army? I don't think so!"

"Well, somebody's got to defend this country," I countered. "And let's remember, I'm eighteen years old now. I can make my own decisions on things like this. I've already signed up, in fact. I leave for basic training in September."

Her face reddened with anger. "I can't believe this. *You've already signed up?* Well, if you're old enough to do something that crazy, you're old enough to find another place to live. Get out!"

"Okay, if that's how you want it," I answered. I had set my course for the future, and I was not going to be talked out of it. I arranged to move in with my dad across town for the summer. He was ambivalent about my plans, but he didn't try to dissuade me.

As the day drew near to head down to Des Moines and catch the plane for Georgia, I found myself feeling the same apprehensions that millions of other young enlistees have felt over the decades. I was pretty much ignorant of what the future held; I didn't know what to expect. I admit that all the unknown factors managed to raise fears within me. As I packed a few clothes and things in a carry-on bag, I felt myself stepping off into the void.

The night before leaving, I said to Dawn, "You know, I don't know if it's going to work now between us. You've still got two years of high school to finish, and I'm going to be a long way away. Maybe we should just break up." I hated to say this, because I was really starting to love her. But it scared me to be in a growing relationship with a girl. I'd been a loner for so long.

"Oh, really? I don't want us to do that," she protested. "I really care about you. I'll still write to you. Don't you want to stay in touch with me?" Her dark eyes were pleading.

"Well, the thing is, I can't even phone you for the first thirteen weeks," I answered. "It's just a big problem. I don't know what I'm getting into. We'd better call it quits."

She reached over to give me a hug. I stiffened, even though a part of me wanted her to still be my girlfriend. We said an awkward good-bye. I got the feeling I hadn't fully convinced her that it was over between us. Actually, I hadn't convinced myself, either.

Twenty-four hours later a group of us stepped off the airplane at Hartsfield International Airport in Atlanta to the worst blast of heat and humidity I had ever felt. *Even my boyhood years in Texas weren't this bad*, I thought. It was like falling into a clothes dryer with a load of wet towels.

On the two-hour bus ride south toward Fort Benning, which was on the Alabama state line, nervous guys tried to smother their apprehensions by one-upping each other with stories of the horrors to come. Somebody's dad had said we'd have to do a hundred push-ups in two minutes, while somebody's uncle had said we'd have to run five miles with a heavy pack in twenty-five minutes. Somebody else claimed that worst of all was the "gas chamber." The drill sergeants would put us in a sealed room and try to kill us with fumes. We'd be bleeding through our eyes, coughing up our intestines, and everything.

I sat there looking out the bus window at the Georgia night and bit my lip. *Man, if it's this bad, I don't know if I'll be able to make it,* I told myself. *They're not even talking about Ranger training. They're just describing step one. Maybe I'll crash and burn right here at the start.*

The minute we stepped off the bus that night, I realized that a week before I had made a stupid mistake regarding my hair. Mr. Walker had said not to worry about getting a haircut because the army would quickly do that job for free. So just for the lark of it, I had stopped by my aunt's beauty shop back in Fort Dodge and said, "Hey, can I have a mohawk? I've always wanted one, and this is a good time."

"Are you sure about that, Jeff?" my aunt had asked.

"Yeah—the army is just going to shave it off anyway." So she granted my wish.

Now I realized upon seeing the steely eyes of my first drill sergeants that I totally stood out from the others in this group—and that was not a good thing. I was the center of attention, which meant I would get "special" treatment from the get-go. *I'm already in trouble,* I thought. *They've got me pegged as a maverick.*

By the next day, of course, I looked like everyone else. I was soon swallowed up in the rigid schedules and protocols and noise and dust and demands of army life. I learned what it was like to give up everything familiar to me and spend every waking second eating, drinking, and speaking army. I watched homesickness spread like wildfire among guys who suffered agonizing withdrawal from TV or the occasional Snickers bar.

But at the end of our first group run of five miles, I found myself thinking, *Hey, that wasn't so bad!* Actually, I had always more or less enjoyed running even back home. I could handle this.

The first time we marched with a forty-pound pack on our backs, I got through it okay. Yes, I had a blister or two, but it wasn't terrible. Next came the obstacle course. When I finished, I thought, *Well, that could have been worse.*

Even the infamous "gas chamber" turned out to be bearable. Every new soldier has to become acquainted with NBC (nuclear/biological/chemical) gear. We suited up in our gas masks and moved into the room. They locked the doors, told us to remove our masks, and then turned on the riot control gas. Some guys did freak out. But it was manageable; the doors opened up again before long. I wouldn't call it fun, nor did I volunteer to go through it a second time. But I survived.

What I was learning about the unknown was that sometimes its advance billing sounds worse than the reality. People say stuff that turns out to be exaggeration. If you just take situations one at a time, stay calm, and cope with what's right in front of you—not what's ballooning inside your imagination—you can get through it. The experience, in fact, can be an opportunity to train for an even greater task down the road.

AGAINST THE ODDS

Late one night on guard duty, I was cleaning the shower stall, mainly to stay awake. Down on my hands and knees, I was scrubbing away with enthusiasm. What I didn't realize was that my drill sergeant was standing behind me in the doorway, watching. He was a man in his middle thirties, with a trademark high-and-tight haircut and a low, raspy voice.

All of a sudden, he asked, "Why ya workin' so hard?" I jumped with surprise.

"Oh!" I exclaimed, swirling around. "I didn't know you were there!"

"The rest of the soldiers on detail are struggling just to keep their eyes open about now," he said. "So why are you in here working?"

I didn't know what to say. Finally I offered, "I guess I just wanted to do my best."

He didn't directly comment. Instead, he asked, "What do you want to do in the army?"

"I want to be an infantryman," I answered quickly. That was the stock reply I had been taught to say for the past weeks.

"No, I mean what do you *really* want to do?"

"Well," I said, then paused for a moment. Should I tell him the truth? "I want to be a Ranger. I want to push myself to the limits."

A smirk rose up across his face. He looked at me as if I'd said about the dumbest thing imaginable.

"You'll never make it," he declared. "You don't have the shape for it. Plus, I didn't see that in your contract when you joined. Chances are you'll never even get to try."

I wasn't sure how to respond. All I could think to say was, "I'm going to do my best."

"Yeah, I'm sure you will," the drill sergeant said as he turned to walk out. I couldn't help noticing that his shoulder bore no Ranger tab. A few hours later, when I had finished guard duty and returned to my bunk, I told myself, *It will be my mission in life to prove him wrong.*

Unfortunately, this conversation with the drill sergeant served to once again single me out from the group. The man delighted thereafter in giving me the most difficult tasks. It was his way of mocking my ambition. *So you're going to be a Ranger one day, huh?* He would look me in the eyes and laugh.

This only served to stiffen my motivation. *You have no idea what I'm capable of,* I thought to myself.

Basic and infantry training wrapped up in early December, and I plunged directly into three weeks of Airborne School, again at Fort Benning. Here, too, I was thrown into something I'd never done before: jumping out of an airplane with a parachute on my back. It wasn't as frightening as it sounds, however; the round parachute is attached to a static line that's tied to the airplane like an umbilical cord. When you reach a certain descent, the line pulls the chute open, and you drift the rest of the way to the ground. You don't have to think or make any decisions. It's little more than a glorified amusement park ride—not at all like free-fall jumping, which would come much later.

And sure enough, Mike Walker's prediction came true. The day arrived when two Rangers in shiny boots and immaculate uniforms showed up to give us their pitch. After a brief description, the magic moment came. "All right, who's interested in becoming a Ranger? Raise your right hand."

I shot up my hand in about 0.05 seconds. Three or four others in my group did the same. The Ranger then told us to show up at a briefing the next night and gave the location.

I could hardly wait to get to the meeting. Fifty or sixty guys from various units were in the room. We listened to more explanations, including the part about RIP—the eighteen-day Ranger Indoctrination Program that would put us to the first tests. At the end of the speeches, we were told to sign a list at the back of the room if we wanted to be sent to RIP. If not, we could just walk out the door and keep going.

I held my breath as I realized I was sitting in a faraway spot and wouldn't get to the sign-up list until nearly everyone had passed it. What if no more spaces were left? *Oh, God, save me a spot!* I was honestly scared that I'd be shut out from my dream.

To my surprise, however, when I got to the paper, only eighteen guys had signed it. I was number nineteen. The other three dozen had quickly decided that Ranger life was not for them after all.

On the final day of Airborne School, all of us who had completed the five required jumps lined up for the time-honored tradition of receiving our wings pin. Anybody who had bought a maroon beret put it on for the first time. It was a proud moment, but what I was most eager to hear was the summons for RIP.

"The following men fall out for transfer to Ranger Indoctrination Program!" came the announcement. The Ranger sergeant then began reading the list of nineteen names, starting with "Adams! Brown! Harris! Jones! Nelson! Rogers!" until he finally got down the alphabet to "Struecker!" I ran across the grass to join the formation. Then glancing left and right, I realized something odd. There weren't nineteen of us here after all. There were only five. The other fourteen, though having initially raised their right hands, gone to the meeting, and signed the list, weren't going to take the plunge. They had lost their will to become a Ranger.

What's with you guys? I said to myself. *I thought you were going to do this. You even talked about it in the barracks. Where are your guts? You're not even going to try?*

My reverie was broken by a new order. "Get your bags and load them on this open truck!" We scrambled for our belongings and then looked around for the bus that would carry us to our new quarters for RIP. There was no bus. The truck started moving, and we were told to run along behind it. Two miles later we arrived at our destination. The stakes were already being raised for those who thought they wanted to be the best.

NOT ALWAYS "FAIR"

RIP was everything I had hoped the army would throw at me, a young and somewhat smart-mouthed teenager. It definitely challenged me physically, mentally, and emotionally. It forced me to pay attention to detail and not be just one of the crowd. I had said I wanted to be part of an elite organization—well, here it was! Guys dropped out like flies—twenty on the very first day. The two hundred or so soldiers were weeded down to about twenty by the end of the program. I was proud to be among them. When I came out I was assigned to the Ranger reconnaissance detachment, still at Fort Benning.

This did not mean I had arrived, however. Yes, I was a Ranger—but on probation, so to speak. Without passing through the gauntlet of Ranger School sometime in the next six months, I wouldn't be staying. I would instead be dumped back into an ordinary infantry unit with those who had never aspired to rise above the rest.

I didn't get my chance until the following October. By now I had been a soldier for thirteen months. My team leader pulled me aside the Sunday before I left to say two last things to me—one encouraging, the other scary. He handed me an extra Ranger tab and said, "Stick this inside your hat. Whenever you feel like quitting, just pull off your hat and look at this tab for a moment. It'll keep you driving on, in spite of how exhausted you are, to win one of these for yourself."

Then his tone turned dramatic. He pointed his finger at my chest and said, "Look, Private—I'm telling you, unless you break your leg or have a death in your family, you *better* finish Ranger school! Either you show up here by Christmas with a Ranger tab on your shoulder, or don't come back to this unit at all. Just keep going on down the road to whatever sorry job the army thinks up for you. But it won't be here, I can assure you of that."

"Yes, Sergeant. I understand." He was dead serious, and I knew it.

I signed in that afternoon along with about 350 other guys, put my stuff away, and actually got a good night's sleep. Early Monday morning began five straight days of physical testing. Every event had a minimum performance standard, and the minute you failed any one of them, you were instantly removed from the group. If you were far below standard, they shipped you back to your unit right away. If you were close, however, you could be "recycled"—segregated from the group and given a chance to start Ranger School again in two weeks. Meanwhile, you led a miserable life over in a separate camp fondly known as "the gulag."

We lined up for the first part of the PT test: sixty push-ups in two minutes. I happened to be within earshot of the instructors as they looked across the field of 350 guys. "They're too many," one of them said. "We'll have to drop about half of them right here." In other words, they had no intention of seeing this many guys through Ranger School. The course couldn't accommodate a class this big. The weeding-out process was in full mode already.

I was petrified. I could just see myself getting tossed out on the very first day. The sergeant's words the morning before reverberated through my brain. *Without a Ranger tab, don't even bother coming back here.*

The command to start push-ups rang across the field, and in groupings of twenty or so we dropped onto our hands to begin. I pumped away with all my might as an instructor counted over my head. My shoulders began to ache as I passed forty, then forty-five. *Just fifteen more,* I told myself. *Keep going, keep going . . .*

Then something weird happened. The instructor's cadence went, "Fifty-four . . . fifty-five . . . fifty-six . . . fifty-seven . . . fifty-eight . . . fifty-nine . . . fifty-nine . . . fifty-nine . . . fifty-nine . . ." *What's wrong? Why was he disqualifying these last push-ups?* I knew I was doing them correctly. I started to panic. Less than ten seconds remained to complete the standard.

I kept pushing with all my might, paying even more attention to my form—straight back, straight elbows at the top of the push-up. Once more, once more—and at the very last second, it seemed, the instructor's voice announced, "Sixty! All right, you're good. Get up, go back to the line."

I gasped with relief as I got to my feet. He had been playing a mind game with me. But I had overcome. I had learned to keep performing even if the circumstance wasn't "fair." On future battlefields, the enemy wasn't always going to fight fair. No use whining about it.

While I was catching my breath, I saw a number of other guys being sent off immediately for not making sixty in two minutes. There wasn't time to watch, however, as the rest of us were ordered to the next event: seventy-two sit-ups in two minutes. This time when the monitor started counting, " . . . seventy-one . . . seventy-one . . . seventy-one . . . seventy-one," I knew what the deal was. But would he let me pass at the last minute like the first guy? I kept straining with everything I had, until he finally counted the last sit-up within the time limit.

The two-mile run was not so frightening for me; again, running was my hobby. I completed this with a comfortable margin of time. The same held true for pull-ups. I got past that one without difficulty.

On subsequent days came the five-mile run in formation through the backwoods of Fort Benning. There also was a set of swim tests: covering fifteen meters with all your equipment on; springing off a three-meter board blindfolded and getting back to the pool edge; jumping in with all your equipment and ditching it in the water, like you'd have to do in an emergency.

The twelve-mile road march while carrying your forty- to fifty-pound rucksack was grueling, because every time a guy in our squad didn't keep up and got banished to the gulag, his equipment was distributed among the rest of us! By the end of the march, the remaining three or four of us must have each been carrying a hundred pounds of gear. Besides my own pack, I ended up with a radio, a machine gun, and blocks of dummy ammunition. Somewhere about mile ten, the right shoulder strap on my pack broke. At that point, I thought I was doomed to fail.

I'm still not sure how I passed that day. By the end of that first week, the instructors had indeed achieved their goal. The 350 men who started now numbered no more than about 160.

NONSTOP EXPEDITION

The main activity for the remaining fifty-three days of Ranger School began on Saturday—a daily mission to accomplish in open country, organized for small units of men such as a squad or platoon. The mission could be to conduct an ambush, do a reconnaissance, or raid a target. Leadership was constantly rotated among us, without much warning. You had to pay attention at all times, because if you were daydreaming, the supervising instructor was sure to say, "Okay, Struecker, you're in charge. You have five minutes to tell me what you're going to do next with this group."

We had a very brief time each morning to plan the day's work. Soon we were off navigating through the terrain toward the objective. There we would fight a mock battle (others played the role of enemy), accomplish our goal, then march again through the night to a designated patrol base. If your squad had good leadership, worked well together, and didn't get lost along the way, you might get two hours of sleep out under the stars. Then before sunrise, the whole thing would start over again.

The first twelve or thirteen days were spent in the pine woods of Fort Benning. Next came an equal stint in the mountains of north Georgia, followed by a third ordeal in the swamps of Eglin Air Force Base in the Florida panhandle—in some ways, this was the worst. Finally, the last twelve or thirteen days happened in desert conditions at Dugway Proving Grounds, Utah.

The whole point was to push our leadership skills, to see how we thought under duress. We were given one MRE (Meals-Ready-to-Eat) per day on most days; once in a while, we got two MREs. The average guy lost a fifth of his body weight during Ranger School.

The lessons I'd learned in basic training—to just keep concentrating on the task at hand and it won't be as tough as you think—now needed a whole second layer. This was absolutely grueling. Your brain could hardly function with so little sleep and so little food. Every mission you led was graded by the accompanying instructor— pass or fail. You had to pass at least half of them or you wouldn't get the Ranger tab in the end.

Plus, the instructor was constantly tempting us to drop out. "You guys hungry? I got some hot coffee and doughnuts over here on the truck. Anybody who wants some, just help yourself. Then the truck can take you back to the barracks, where it's nice and warm. They got real beds there, too, you know."

I'd grit my teeth and turn the other direction, ignoring him.

The first mission I led did not go particularly well. I made a number of tactical mistakes that put my men in jeopardy. When it was over, the instructor glared at me and said, "That was as bad as I've ever seen in my life."

I wasn't sure about the consequences, though. "So, did I pass?"

He looked at me like I was an idiot. "Uh—no," he grunted and walked away.

The next mission a few days later wasn't much better. Once again, I failed. The specter of going home from Ranger School in shame loomed like a thundercloud over my head. I had virtually no more margin for error.

The test I'll never forget was Thanksgiving night. I was the designated leader for a patrol through the swamps that would take about twelve hours. By now our original group of sixteen or eighteen guys was down to half a dozen. It was raining.

We'd already marched for hours. In the darkness I pulled out my rubber poncho, threw it over my head, and called the guys to huddle under it with me for a five-minute briefing. I aimed my red-lens flashlight at the map and started talking. "Okay, here's where we are right now—and here's where we've got to get before we can stop for the night . . ." We were all absolutely miserable in the cold drizzle.

Suddenly I heard sniffling from the guy next to me. I thought, *Well, maybe he's just cold; he's got a runny nose.* Then the guy on the other side started sniffling, too. I raised the flashlight to sweep around the faces, and there were brimming eyes all over the place. A couple of guys started outright boo-hooing.

"What's the matter with you guys?" I snapped. "What's going on?" I didn't get it.

"It's Thanksgiving, man," somebody replied. "I want to be home with my family tonight."

"Yeah," another chimed in. "My wife is all by herself right now— on a holiday. This is stupid."

The dam broke at that point. Guys started telling how good their mom's turkey and gravy was, and here we were out in the rain starving to death. It turned into a full-scale pity party right there under my poncho. The whole situation was spiraling out of control.

The main thought in my head was: *How in the world am I going to get these guys to do what they're supposed to do in the next thirty minutes? If I don't think of something quick, I'm going to fail this patrol assignment—and that will be it for Ranger School. I'll be dead.* It wouldn't be my fault personally—but as everyone knows, the buck stops with the leader.

God, what am I going to do? I silently prayed. *I have to pass this patrol. How do I motivate these guys to get their heads back into the immediate task at hand?*

At that point, I remembered something I could use for a bribe. Days before, I had deliberately gone hungry in order to stash an MRE in the bottom of my pack just in case I got totally desperate sometime. Everybody knew I had it. Guys had even offered me their credit card number if I'd give it to them.

"Men, listen up," I said. "I'll let you share my emergency MRE, okay? Here you go." I went digging through my stuff to produce the precious meal, which they wolfed down in about two seconds.

"Now—let me tell you something for real. In just a couple more days, we're outta here. On the flight to Utah for the last stage, we know they're going to give us a decent meal—if you make it that far, you understand? So buck up and do what has to be done."

One guy still would not stop crying softly. "Hey," I said to him with a touch of sarcasm, "do you see a pay phone around here, so you can call home? No. Do you see a mailbox? Not exactly. You can cry all night long, but it's not going to do any good. I can't do anything to change the situation, and neither can you. It is what it is."

By the grace of God they all, with a little bit of food in their stomachs, stepped up to the job that miserable night. We clawed through our physical, mental, and emotional exhaustion to hit the trail again, marching through the rain until we reached our base around four in the morning. I can't tell you how relieved I was a few hours later when the supervising instructor said, "Okay, Struecker, you passed that one."

Four weeks later, on December 22, 1988, I stood on the parade field at Fort Benning to receive my Ranger tab. At six feet one, I was down to 145 pounds. I felt proud of having survived, as well as a huge sense of relief that I could go back to my unit and face my sergeant again.

I looked around and counted the graduates: there were just 54 of us out of the 350 who had started Ranger School. Actually, less than that, because some of the 54 were "recycles" from earlier classes who finally made it on the second or third try.

Other men had invited special people in their lives to come to this ceremony and pin on their tab. I had not done so—and now wished I had. I wanted Dawn there to see me. She had no clue what I had endured the last fifty-eight days. Oh, well—a missed opportunity.

To a civilian reader, I suppose all this grunting and torment sounds excessive. Some people think army trainers are just a bunch of sadists who get their kicks out of making other human beings suffer. But the truth is I would need every bit of this discipline and determination in the future. I had to rise above my fear of the unknown and the unpredictable in order to be effective later on, when the enemies were real and the bullets were live. I had not yet seen the worst of life's challenges by far.

Captain Jeff Struecker with Corporal Palmer (also a member of the Ranger Reconnaissance Detachment) on an U.S. Air Force C-141 Starlifter hours before the Rangers Operations in Kuwait.

Four

FIRST BLOOD

A YEAR PASSED, AND ONCE AGAIN THE CHRISTMAS SEASON came around. Much of the year for us Rangers had been spent on two-hour recall status, which meant we could not travel more than two hours away from Fort Benning. The call to grab our gear and deploy to some hot spot in the world could come at any time.

More and more, the name Panama kept coming up. The United States government was fairly unhappy with the actions of strongman Manuel Noriega: his abuse of human rights (including the thirty-five thousand Americans who lived there), his nullifying of an election after his party lost, his up-to-the-elbows involvement in drug trafficking. Like most Americans, my knowledge about the country of Panama was not much more than that it had a canal, was somewhere in Central America, and the people spoke Spanish. But I learned a little more every time we were summoned to head that way. Then at the last minute, the mission would be scrubbed.

On the Saturday night of December 16, 1989, I was on Charge-of-Quarters duty in our Ranger barracks. My job was to answer the phones and keep the building secure. I just recently had been promoted to sergeant. As the hours slowly passed, I flipped through the thick file of leave papers, making sure all was in order for guys heading home for the holidays. Naturally I made sure *my* form was there, duly filled out and signed. I noticed the form for Command Sergeant Major Mariano Leon-Guerrero. Eventually I even came to Colonel William F. "Buck" Kernan's form; he was commander of the whole Ranger Regiment. Both of them were to depart the next morning. This place was due to get fairly quiet in the coming week.

Eventually my shift ended, and I headed to my bunk to get a few hours of sleep. I couldn't wait for the Christmas break to come, when I would head back to my family in Iowa.

Then came a knock on my door. I opened it to hear these words: "The balloon just went up. We're going to war."

Oh, really? I walked downstairs to the common area, where guys were talking about how this was probably just another false alarm— another training exercise to see if we were truly ready to deploy.

But no, I told myself as I thought back to the papers I'd studied last night, *that doesn't make sense. They wouldn't mess up the Christmas plans of the highest Ranger commander just for a drill. This must be the real deal.*

"A Marine officer got shot and killed in Panama yesterday," somebody said. "President Bush [meaning Bush Sr.] has had enough. We're actually going this time. We have to get our stuff together in twenty-four hours."

This was, in fact, an almost leisurely pace for Rangers. Normally a Ranger unit could be loaded and flying, wheels off the ground, in eighteen hours. The job had even been done once or twice in as little as nine.

I was a radio telephone operator in the reconnaissance detachment, so I got busy checking out my gear, making sure it was ready to transmit back and forth to the satellite. I packed my rucksack, helped pull ammunition from our stock, and reviewed plans with my superiors. The PDF (Panamanian Defense Forces) would give us a fight—that was for sure. We, along with the Fifth and Seventh Infantry divisions, the Eighty-second Airborne, several Marine units, and others, would storm the airfields first, spread out from there to other military installations, and ultimately seek to capture Noriega himself. We'd launch a quick but massive strike under the name "Operation Just Cause."

INTO THE FRAY

I finished packing sometime that Monday afternoon and still had several hours before we all reported to the airfield. I went back to my room to wait. Sitting there on my bunk, my mind began to buzz. *So what happens if I die in this invasion?* I had not thought seriously about dying since my commitment to Christ at age thirteen. Now as a twenty-year-old, I sensed no fear. I wondered if that was odd. Maybe I *should* be afraid, given what I was heading into. But I was not.

I did think, however, that I should write a letter to my father, just in case I didn't come back. I pulled out a piece of paper. I told him I very much loved him and the rest of the family, and if something happened to me, I hoped he would be proud of what I had done for my country. I asked him to be sure and take good care of my beloved Mustang. Then I folded up the letter, put it in an envelope with his name and address, and left it on my desk for someone to find.

I wonder what Dawn's doing today, I mused next. *She's expecting me home for Christmas. What if I don't show up?* Rangers were not allowed to tell their loved ones in advance where they were heading. Only afterward could the details come out. *Man, I hope this goes okay,* I thought, *because I really want to get to know Dawn better.*

This mood of reflection came to an abrupt halt when it was time to head for the airfield that night. The First Ranger Battalion arrived from its base at Hunter Army Airfield, Savannah, Georgia, while the Second Ranger Battalion flew in all the way from Fort Lewis, Washington, outside Tacoma. I looked across the vast array of vehicles, weaponry, ammunition, and people, and gasped; it was more firepower than I'd seen in one place at one time in my whole career. There were brand-new AH-64 Apache attack helicopters with their Hellfire missiles, ready to be used for the first time in combat. The place literally swarmed with military might.

The hour was late when we loaded onto C-141 Starlifters and rumbled off into the darkness, headed for Howard Air Force Base, a U.S. facility inside the Panama Canal Zone. On the seven-hour flight, I started worrying about how I would react if I got into a real firefight. Would I do what my leaders expected me to do? Or would I let down my friends, my unit? Would I embarrass my country?

God, please don't let that happen, I prayed. *If I get hurt or whatever, that's okay. But I just don't want to disappoint the people who are depending on me.*

We stepped off the plane the next morning into the muggy, tropical air of Panama. All day Tuesday was spent getting ready for the actual assault. At 0100 hours early Wednesday, December 20, my Ranger buddies began dropping onto Torrijos-Tucumen International Airport as well as Rio Hato Airfield about forty miles south on the Pacific coast, knocking down the Panamanian forces in both places and taking charge. About forty-five minutes later, the famous Eighty-second

Airborne from Fort Bragg began parachuting down at Torrijos-Tocumen. Meanwhile, the latest specimen of U.S. military technology, the F-117A stealth bomber, came silently streaking toward the heart of Panama City, undetected by radar, to drop a two-thousand-pound bomb.

AC-130 Spectre gunships were raking La Comandancia, the Panamanian military headquarters in the city, as well. You could feel the ground shake all the way out to Howard Air Force Base. The night sky glowed orange. Despite antiaircraft fire, our forces ruled the skies within minutes.

My reconnaissance group waited on the sidelines until orders came around 4:30 in the morning to start picking up casualties from both major airfields. Combat on the ground had been stiff throughout the night, and a number of guys were hurt, either from enemy fire or from injuries while parachuting down. About ten or twelve of us—my team plus a couple of Air Force special operators and some others—took off for Rio Hato in a CH-53 helicopter. We landed near the casualty collection point.

When the ramp came down, I was surprised to see twenty-five or so troops needing evacuation. Most of them had broken an arm, a shoulder, or a leg when their main parachute malfunctioned. They had dropped out of the sky with just five hundred feet of altitude, leaving no time to use their reserve chutes. The medics had them already bandaged up and waiting; some were even carrying their own IVs.

A couple of the men had sustained shots from the PDF, but these wounds were already packed full of dressing, and the bleeding was controlled.

"Let's go, guys!" I hollered to the group. "Jump aboard." This many people would pretty much max out the CH-53, which had a capacity of no more than about forty.

The rotors were still spinning when I learned that Staff Sergeant Larry Bernard, one of our most experienced Rangers, was hurt far worse than the others. A doctor and a physician's assistant (PA) were desperately working to keep him alive after a rocket had exploded at close range. To be honest, both arms had been blown off, as well as one leg, and there was massive trauma to his back. His chest had been opened up, and Captain Donovan, one of the best PAs in Ranger history, had his hands inside the man's chest massaging away to keep his heart pumping. Yet Bernard was going downhill fast.

Where was I going to find room for this man and his two attendants? Every square foot was already occupied.

On the wall of the helicopter, about five feet up, was a set of brackets for suspending a stretcher. "Move aside!" I ordered the wounded already on board. "We have to put this guy up on the wall!" We loaded Larry Bernard into place, while Donovan never stopped his CPR.

I was about to signal the loadmaster that he could close the gate now when a voice on the ground called, "Wait a minute! We got bodies over here, too!"

"What are you talking about?" I yelled. "I thought we got everybody!"

"No. We've got five body bags." These were Rangers who had been killed by hostile fire throughout the night.

Three others and I jumped off the aircraft to run to where the six long, green rubber bags with large zippers lay. All of them were smeared on the outside with blood from the hurried effort of putting the body inside. In that moment I did not freak out, even though this was certainly the closest to death and blood I had experienced. My mind was too consumed with, *Where in the world am I going to put them?*

Each bag had four handles for lifting. One by one we brought the bodies to the helicopter ramp. I started motioning to several of the less seriously wounded. "Get off for just a minute," I ordered. "We may not be able to take you on this run after all. If not, we'll come back for you." They moved out on to the ground as I had requested, and we began stacking the body bags aboard like cordwood.

I could not help noticing that the fifth bag was much lighter than the previous four. I knew what that meant. There wasn't a lot of body left to take home.

In the end, we managed to cram all the wounded back on to the CH-53. I'm still not sure how the space was found. Several of us jumped onto the ramp at the last minute, as the loadmaster hit the hydraulic lever to raise it.

Unfortunately, he didn't realize that a guy with a broken leg had his leg stuck in the hinge. He screamed out fast enough to stop the loadmaster, who lowered the ramp again. "Looks like we're going to have to fly with it open," the man said. Most of us had done this kind of thing before; it just meant snapping the safety line around our waists into a hook on the wall or in the floor and holding on tightly.

The helicopter lifted off the ground—slowly. Right away I could tell we were terribly overweight. This bird would be a big fat target barely moving across the landscape.

Within twenty seconds, Panamanian soldiers in the jungle below were taking shots at us. This was my first experience at receiving enemy fire. I couldn't tell which direction it was coming from, but I knew it was for real. We all huddled or sprawled out hoping the bullets wouldn't hit anything essential on this big, lumbering bird.

Maybe this is it for me, I thought. *Maybe I won't get the chance to go back and see Dawn again.*

Soon our pilot began twisting and turning as best he could, doing evasive maneuvers. Back where we were, guys were tossed left and right. Everybody was hanging on and holding their breath.

Then the bird lurched suddenly—and Larry Bernard's stretcher came crashing down off the wall! People screamed; the two medical personnel went flying and then scrambled back to his side as fast as they could. As for me, I happened to be sitting in just the wrong spot. When Larry fell, all the bile and blood in his chest cavity came splashing across my lap. It was as if somebody had turned over a bucket on me.

The smell of the fluids hit my nose with full force. At almost the same moment, I got an additional whiff of the plane's jet exhaust, since the ramp was open. The combination of the two stenches instantly made me nauseous.

For the rest of the flight back to our base, I couldn't worry about getting shot down by enemy groundfire; I was too preoccupied with the fear of throwing up in front of all these Rangers. If I did, I knew I would never hear the end of it. *God, please don't let me embarrass myself in front of these guys!* I pleaded. *They'll never let me live it down.*

For some reason that prayer was answered. The minute we landed, I jumped off and moved away from the helicopter for a breath of fresh air. With that my head cleared and my stomach calmed down. Soon I was back to help move body bags toward a waiting chaplain. The injured soldiers were at the same time hustled toward the medical treatment area.

No more than ten minutes elapsed before the word was passed: Larry Bernard was dead. The medics had heroically fought to keep him alive, but in the end, this good man was lost. I stopped to grieve the fact that within hours his family back in the States, like those of the other five, would be getting a terrible knock on their door.

This was my first hard lesson in the fact that war—for all its necessity—is a nasty business. My passion to serve my country on the cutting edge of battle could exact a heavy price. General Dwight Eisenhower said, "History does not long entrust the care of freedom to the weak or the timid"—or, I might add, to those averse to blood. We all wish this were not part of the endeavor, but it is.

ALAMO IN THE JUNGLE

During the next couple of days, our detachment went on several other missions, including the rescue of a U.S. covert operative being held at a prison camp. Flying back on a Black Hawk helicopter, the enemy fire was intense enough that we had to land in an open field. The crew checked out the tail section while many of us guarded them with weapons raised to our noses. They found plenty of bullet holes, but the rotor was still functional. So we made it back to base safely after all.

The most vivid encounter for me, however, didn't happen until the following Sunday, which was Christmas Eve. We were sent to take and control an airfield in the far west of the country, almost on the Costa Rican border. When our CH-47 helicopters landed, we found a few Panamanian soldiers on the ground. They quickly scattered.

As evening fell we got reports that a large number of PDF personnel were massing outside the gates—perhaps a thousand or more. If they attacked, the two dozen or so of us would not be able to handle them. We radioed for reinforcements.

Soon an entire company from Second Ranger Battalion arrived, along with some special operations forces and others. We set up a perimeter all around this field, which was nothing more than a bald hilltop in the middle of the jungle. We then waited. When would the attack come?

With all the CH-47s flying in and out of the same area, there was a mishap when two helicopters got too close to each other. The exhaust of the one in front threw the second one off balance and forced an emergency landing, causing major damage to the front engine and rotor. No one was injured, but upon inspection the crews determined the second bird could not fly in this condition. It would need an entire new front engine.

The thought of just abandoning this aircraft was never considered; it was a multimillion-dollar special-ops helicopter. We were not about to leave it behind for the enemy.

We began to realize some of us would have to hold this airfield overnight, until the maintenance personnel could bring in the replacement engine and install it. Wouldn't you know, my team of seven was tapped to guard the field as the hours of Christmas Eve ticked by, while the rest of the force helicoptered out to head for more urgent missions. But what about the thousand PDF lurking in the jungle? Were they still there, or had they gone home? Nobody knew.

We got busy setting defenses. We booby-trapped the downed helicopter both outside and in, so that anyone going inside would trigger an enormous ball of flame. The fuel lines, oil lines, and hydraulic lines were all wired to explode. We placed Claymore mines around the airfield. At various strategic locations we set up and loaded grenade launchers that could be fired in an instant.

I was glad for the leadership of dark-haired Sergeant First Class Joe Ulibarri, an experienced man with exceptional endurance ability. In spite of his average build, he had run ultramarathons (fifty kilometers and beyond) and seemed invincible. He put a couple of men in the field's control tower, where they could get a higher angle of vision on any invaders. The rest of us at ground level faced outward, watching the night. I heard the clicks as a couple of guys flipped their weapon levers from safe to semiautomatic, ready to unleash a hail of bullets.

Most of us had slept less than four hours during the past three days. But nobody was nodding off. Sometime past eleven o'clock, as I stared intently through a set of night-vision goggles, I noticed what I did *not* want to see: movement on the dirt road alongside the airfield. At first it looked like just a dozen or so people. *We could handle that many*, I told myself. Then it seemed more like fifty . . . then a hundred . . . then even more. My heart began to race. This would be the Alamo for us. We would have to fight here until our deaths. But we would take down as many of the enemy with us as possible.

I kept peering into the darkness—and noticed an odd thing. Through the goggle lenses I could make out the shapes of the growing crowd of people moving along, but I failed to see their weapons. Where were the guns? Had the PDF managed to hide them from view somehow? It didn't make sense.

I looked down at my watch; it was now 11:40 p.m. Eleven forty on Christmas Eve. Suddenly it hit me: *This is Panama—a strongly Catholic country. What do Catholics do late on Christmas Eve? They go to midnight Mass!* I squinted tightly at the figures in my view. They weren't soldiers after all. There were women along with the men; there were little kids, old grandmas—these were villagers going to church!

"Hold on!" I hissed to my fellow soldiers. "I don't think these are enemy after all. I think they're just ordinary civilians going to church!"

"*What?*" team leader Ulibarri shot back. "What are you talking about?"

"Sergeant, it's Christmas Eve," I said. "They're just a bunch of people heading for midnight Mass like they do every year. That's why they're not carrying any weapons."

We all heaved a sigh. How close we had come to a horrible mistake that would have taken scores of innocent lives. We lowered our weapons and regrouped, as the adrenalin levels in each of us drifted back down to normal range.

All through the rest of that night and into Christmas Day, we kept our vigil for any other activity in the jungle. No PDF force ever showed up, however, to try to push us off that hilltop. We had lots of time to think about the responsibility that went with our incredible technology. We could deal out a withering barrage of death and destruction in all directions, but our weapons certainly could not sort out who deserved to get hit and who should be spared. That lay in our human power of discretion. If we were careless even for a moment, extraordinary tragedy could result. Not to mention a huge scandal in the international political arena.

The mechanical crew didn't arrive with the new engine until the following day, December 26. They got the bird ready to fly again, while we continued to stand guard. We were one tired, hungry, but happy squad when we finally lifted off to return to Howard Air Force Base.

A NEW MISSION

By New Year's Eve, Operation Just Cause was winding down. Noriega was in the process of surrendering, and I found myself on a plane heading home. As I looked out the window of that aircraft, I thought,

Tomorrow will be the first day of 1990—the start of a new decade. I get to go on living after all. Panama was not the end of the line for me.

I looked forward to getting back to my familiar room at Fort Benning. When I walked in, there on the dresser was my letter to my dad, still waiting. I picked it up, opened it, and read it again. It triggered within me a powerful reminder to take care of things left undone. For example, I hadn't told my family often enough that I really did love them.

Most urgently, I knew in that moment what I needed to do with my next paycheck. I would head to downtown Columbus, Georgia, to the nearest jeweler and buy a diamond ring. As soon as I could get a weekend pass, I would jump on a plane for Iowa to talk to a very special young lady. No more stalling. Life was too tenuous to procrastinate any longer.

Dawn and Jeff Struecker minutes after arriving in Fort Benning, Georgia, after the men of Bravo Company, 3rd Ranger Battalion returned from months of combat operations in Somalia.

Five

Iowa Bride

"Sir, I have a question for you," I said to my commander not long after bringing the ring back to my room and tucking it away inside a sock in my dresser drawer. "As you know, none of us got to see our family over Christmas because we were in Panama. Could I get a pass one of these weekends for a quick trip home?"

"Yes, that's reasonable, unless we're on two-hour recall," he replied. "Fill out the paperwork, and I'll sign it."

By now Dawn was halfway through her first year of business school in Davenport, Iowa, on the Mississippi River. But she would be traveling the 235 miles back to Fort Dodge in March for the wedding of her older sister, Wendy. This afforded the perfect opportunity for me to show up in town without raising her suspicions.

I knew Dawn loved me, and I loved her—but the seriousness of marriage truly scared me. Such a big step! I had made up my mind, even before meeting Dawn during high school, that if I ever got married, I'd do it once and only once—for life. I wanted no part of the painful trail my mother had walked. By now she had married and divorced *again*—for the fifth time. I was determined to get it right.

Dawn as well had never really known her biological father. He left when she was very young, and she had grown up with her mom and a stepfather. I knew the subject of marriage was as sobering to her as it was to me.

That day in the church for Wendy's wedding, I watched wide-eyed as Dawn came down the aisle in her purple bridesmaid's dress. She was absolutely stunning! Her dark hair set off her glowing face, and she gave me a big smile on her way by my row. It wasn't hard to imagine what she would look like when it got to be *our* turn. Needless to say, I was inspired.

The ceremony ended at last, and we moved toward a jovial reception at a banquet hall in the middle of a park. People congratulated Wendy and Scott, enjoyed the food, and sat telling stories to one another. I waited for the opportune moment, silently calculating what I was about to do. After all, in just thirty-six hours I had to get back on the plane for Georgia.

The festivities began slowing down, and the reception crowd started to dwindle. Now was the time. Moving close to Dawn, I murmured, "Hey, I need to talk to you about something. Could we maybe just cut out for a little bit and go to your house? We can come right back."

She looked at me quizzically. "Right now?" she asked. "What's the matter?"

"Nothing," I said with a smile. "I just want to talk to you, and we don't have a lot of time this weekend."

She paused another second and then said, "Okay."

We went out to my blue Mustang, which I had stored at my dad's, and drove the ten minutes to her mom's place at the edge of town. The house was deserted, of course. We went into the living room.

She stood there in the middle of the floor for a minute, still looking gorgeous in her wedding attire. I sank down on one knee. (We Rangers get right to the point.)

Pulling the ring box out of my pocket, I held my voice steady as I asked, "Dawn, will you be my wife?"

Her face froze. She was absolutely stunned. She couldn't say a word.

I waited. Her eyes went to the diamond ring, then to me, then back to the ring. Still she was mute.

Seconds kept passing. The longer she stood there motionless, the more nervous I became. *This is not going well*, I told myself. *Maybe I've misjudged her interest in me all this time.*

Finally I could stand it no longer. "Um, is this a yes or a no?" I asked. "I'm looking for an answer here."

That broke the ice. "Yes, of course I'll marry you!" she finally cried, reaching out to me. I quickly stood up to embrace her. We laughed and squeezed each other as we swirled around. I was relieved to find out that she wasn't hesitant about marriage to me; my odd timing had just caught her off guard, immobilizing her for a bit.

We needed to talk about a ton of new things now—but we also needed to get back to Wendy's reception. Five minutes later we were back in the car. At the party Dawn quickly told her twin sister, Diane, what had just occurred. There was a shriek, and soon Diane was calling for the crowd's attention to announce the happy news, as Dawn proudly showed off her ring to her family.

I felt warm inside. This was going to be great. God had led me to the woman who would make my life complete. Hopefully I could do the same for her.

Monday morning I was on the plane for Fort Benning, without the time for conversation that we wanted. We hadn't even set a date yet. All of that would have to be sorted out on the phone in the coming weeks and months.

Prep Time

After we both had caught our breath and studied the calendar, we settled on April 20, 1991, for our wedding—thirteen months down the road. I would be twenty-two years old and she would be twenty. We would get married in Fort Dodge and then begin married life in Georgia—assuming I was still assigned there.

I tried to be realistic with her about the unusual life of an army wife. I pointed out that my job was definitely not nine-to-five. Rangers especially were subject to sudden surprises. I repeated to Dawn the old saying among soldiers: "If the army had wanted you to have a wife, they'd have issued you one along with your boots and your weapon."

"Yes, I know," she answered sweetly. "But I love you, and I know we'll make it work."

I told her about the support programs for married soldiers and how army spouses banded together to help one another through frequent moves and unpredictable deployments. I also said, "I'll make you a promise. You as my wife will always take priority over the United States Army. At any point in my career, if you find it too difficult for me to do what I've been ordered to do, you have veto authority. I'll get a change of assignment—or I'll even leave the service if necessary. You come first."

"Okay, you've got a deal!" she replied with a laugh. "I really appreciate that."

As the months passed, wedding plans began taking shape. We

talked on the phone almost every night. Excitement was mounting. We figured out how to sign up for premarital counseling in two different places eleven hundred miles apart. She would see a clergyman in Iowa while I went to one of the chaplains at Fort Benning.

About halfway through our engagement, on August 2, 1990, something began brewing half a world away that threatened our happy plan. On that day, Saddam Hussein's army pushed across the border into Kuwait. The world community—not just Western nations but others, too, including even those of the Arab League—found this unacceptable. Diplomatic pressure was applied to get Saddam to back off.

As we all remember now, it didn't work.

The Ranger Regiment went back on two-hour recall status. If force were needed, we would almost certainly be called to apply it. After all, "Rangers Lead the Way." We watched the intensifying developments day after day and stayed alert, waiting for orders. We grimaced at reports of how the Iraqi army was brutalizing the Kuwaiti people. This would definitely have to be stopped, one way or another. Operation Desert Shield went into action with various army, navy, marine, and air force units deploying to Saudi Arabia and other Gulf locations. But the Rangers were not summoned—yet.

I chose not to fret about this on the phone with Dawn, and she didn't bring it up. We kept moving forward with our plans. I'd been through enough false alarms that I knew not to borrow worry from tomorrow. I sent Dawn money to reserve the reception site. I lined up a great honeymoon trip to the Caribbean.

Even when the direct air attack cut loose on January 17, 1991, turning Desert Shield into Desert Storm and involving personnel from more than two dozen nations, we remained steady. I held my breath in the barracks with the other guys as we watched CNN, riveted to the footage of Baghdad buildings blowing to bits. I hoped my wedding plans weren't about to get blown up, too. A week passed, then two. The calendar turned to February, with fighter jets raining devastation onto Iraq from the skies.

On Sunday, February 24, the ground war began. Our wedding was just eight weeks away. The regimental staff finally made a clear announcement: "The following units [including mine] are going to go several days from now. You will be gone for a long period of time. You need to prepare yourself and your family." This level of detail was unheard of for a Ranger notice.

I stood there in the briefing room of the Ranger headquarters building staring into space, trying to soak in all the implications. It was now certain that I'd be missing my own wedding! I shook my head in disbelief. How would I ever tell Dawn? The invitations were already addressed, stamped, and ready to drop into the mail. She had already paid for her dress. The bridesmaid dresses were being finalized. The only items left on our list to purchase were the wedding cake and the flowers.

I went back to my room to think. What wretched timing! I tried to put words together for the phone call I knew I had to make, and they wouldn't fit.

I decided to practice first on my dad. I dialed his number.

"Dad, this is Jeff. Something really lousy has happened. I'm being sent out to the Gulf in just a few days—which totally messes up my wedding in April."

"Wow, son. That's too bad."

"I haven't even called Dawn yet. I'm trying to figure out how to tell her."

I could tell the crisis wasn't totally sinking in. My dad had never served in the military and didn't grasp the intensity of my current job. He didn't seem to have any ideas to offer. I soon hung up the phone, dreading the next call.

I waited until evening, when I knew Dawn would be home. She had just finished business school and was back living with her mom.

"Hi, honey—how are you? How was your day?" I began with fake cheerfulness.

She told me several things that had happened. I kept stalling. We chatted about casual stuff for probably fifteen minutes, my heart rate steadily rising.

Finally I had to get on with it. "Dawn, uh, I have to tell you— well, some things have just changed here in the regiment. They made an announcement today—and I'm pretty sure I'm not going to be here on our wedding day."

"*What?*"

"It looks like I'm going to be deployed to the Gulf."

The line went silent as she absorbed this awful news.

"How soon will you be back?" she asked in a hesitant voice.

"I don't know. They never tell you those things, of course. But I'd have to say it would be nowhere close to April 20."

There was another long pause. Was she gearing up to say, *Then forget it!* or *I hate the army!* or what?

With remarkable strength of mind, she declared, "Then we need to get married right away!"

I let out a sigh of relief. "Okay," I said. "Like, how soon do you want to do this?"

"How soon are you leaving?"

"Again, I don't know. It could be as soon as the end of this week or the first part of next week."

"Then we need to get married this weekend!" she announced.

I thought later about an action movie that had come out the previous year—*Navy SEALs*, starring Charlie Sheen. Dawn and I had seen it together. It included a scene where a guy on the SEAL team was getting married. He and his bride were already at the altar, when suddenly a flock of pagers went off. Something in the world had broken loose, and the team all had to leave immediately. The navy guys all ran out of the church, leaving the wedding ceremony unfinished.

The guy was killed on the mission. The movie showed his mother and the fiancée going to his military funeral, where full honors were rolled out. At the end of the funeral, the officer presented the folded American flag to the *mother*, not the young woman, who after all was not quite yet the guy's wife. She was terribly distraught, of course.

I remembered that Dawn was deeply affected by that movie. Now I wondered if that image were still in the back of her mind, driving her urgency in our circumstance.

THROUGH ICE AND SNOW AND GLOOM OF NIGHT

Whatever her motivation, I wanted to get married, too. Back I went to my commander a second time—similar to a year before—asking for a weekend pass. He studied the unit's schedule for deployment and then said okay.

The flurry of activity for Dawn that week was incredible—calling reception managers and food vendors and everybody else to slam together a 2:00 p.m. wedding on *this coming* Saturday, March 2! People gasped and then got to work helping her pull it off.

On that Wednesday, President George H. W. Bush announced that due to the amazing success on the ground, he was calling a cease-fire as of midnight Kuwaiti time. The Iraqi army was in full retreat, and the allies would not push all the way to Baghdad after all. The Hundred-Hour War, as it came to be known, would stand down.

Of course, that didn't say anything definitive about changing the Ranger Regiment's status. So far as I, a lowly sergeant, knew, I was still slated to go for whatever mop-up work remained to be done. The wedding rush would continue.

I jumped on a flight out of Columbus, Georgia, on Friday. This certainly wasn't the way either one of us had expected to come to the happiest day of our lives. But we would see it through regardless.

You would think that nothing else could go wrong—but it did. As we neared Chicago's O'Hare Field, where I would change planes for Des Moines, the pilot came on the intercom to say, "We've got a major ice storm here in the upper Midwest, ladies and gentlemen. There's a chance we might have to divert to a secondary airport. I'll keep you posted." *Oh, no! What if I missed my connection?* I gripped the armrest in annoyance.

The aircraft managed to land at O'Hare in spite of the wicked weather. Inside the terminal, we were soon notified that the airport was closing down for the night. No further takeoffs would be permitted.

I ran for the customer service desk along with hundreds of other frustrated people. "How do I get to Des Moines?" I barked when I got to the head of the line. "I'm getting married *tomorrow!*"

"I'm really sorry, sir," the woman replied. "But there are simply no options for Des Moines tonight. Here's a voucher to give you a break on the price of a hotel room across the street. The first flight I can get you on, *if* the weather improves overnight . . . ," she continued, punching keys on her computer, "is at 7:30 tomorrow morning. That would put you into Des Moines at 8:45. Remember, that's only if the runways are cleared and the right planes are here for deicing and ready to fly."

Should I make a mad dash for the car rental desks and see if I could get a set of wheels to drive through the night to Iowa? Yes, but as a twenty-two-year-old single guy with a not-exactly-perfect driving record, I knew I wouldn't be the most favorite customer for Hertz or Avis—especially in the middle of an ice storm. I was almost sure to be turned down.

By now Dawn was already at the Des Moines airport waiting to meet me, so I couldn't phone her. I did manage to reach her mom and tell her the name of the hotel where I would be stuck overnight. In a little while, Dawn called me there.

"Honey, where are you?" she implored.

"Stuck in an ice storm at O'Hare in Chicago! I can't even get out of here till tomorrow morning."

"That's awful!" she cried. "What are we going to do?"

"We just have to hope the weather clears."

"I know—since I'm already here in Des Moines, I'll jump on Interstate 80 and just drive to Chicago to pick you up!" she said enthusiastically.

"Honey, think about that a minute. It's at least a six-hour drive even on *good* roads, let alone slick pavement."

"Yeah, you're right. We shouldn't try that. Let's just hope the airline thing works out tomorrow morning."

She returned to Fort Dodge. Neither one of us got solid sleep that night for worrying about the next day's travel. My poor bride had worked so hard to reschedule this wedding, and now even the weather seemed to be conspiring against us. The next morning at the airport the airlines were still digging out, and my flight was delayed several times. The Des Moines weather wasn't much better. I landed there around ten in the morning. Dawn gladly picked me up, and we had plenty to talk about on the drive north to Fort Dodge. This normally takes an hour and a half, but with the ice and snow we were on the road considerably longer.

When the magic hour of 2:00 p.m. struck, there I was in my crisp military dress greens, standing at the altar with my brother-in-law at my side as best man, waiting for the processional of the most wonderful woman in the world. The audience was small—basically our two families. But we were getting married!

My mind raced as I stood there waiting for the service to begin. *I hope I'm making the right move here. Am I going to be the husband she truly wants to live with? Will this be a relationship that lasts the rest of our lives? Do we have what it takes to make this marriage work?* I was pretty sure the answers were yes, but in that moment my thoughts still bounced back to my parents' failure—and I was scared. I knew how to execute complicated military missions. But would I succeed at this, the most special mission on earth for me?

Then the music swelled, the doors at the rear of the sanctuary opened, and Dawn appeared in her wedding dress. She was absolutely spectacular! In that instant, all fear vanished. I watched her slowly glide down the center aisle, and I was overwhelmed with joy and hope. *I get to marry this person!* I told myself almost giddily. I was suddenly the most privileged and confident man alive. I was also incredibly grateful.

A NEW DAY

Twenty-four hours later, the weather had cleared, and I was back on a plane for Georgia—alone. It absolutely killed us to admit that bringing Dawn down to Fort Benning just as I shipped out to Kuwait didn't make good sense. It was better for her to stay in Iowa until we could see what my future held. Our cold plunge into the realities of army marriage was tough to handle.

Back on duty Monday, the order to load up for the Gulf did not come. Tuesday was quiet as well. Wednesday passed, then Thursday, then Friday. Plans to deploy were rumored, and then dismissed. As it turned out, the Rangers were kept on hold for weeks, stretching on toward summer.

We continued our training as always, staying in a high state of readiness. Sometimes we would go elsewhere in the United States for specialized maneuvers. But the big airlift to the Middle East did not materialize.

Around Easter I flew home to rent a U-Haul truck and bring Dawn and our things to Fort Benning. We moved into a second-floor apartment in Columbus and started our life together. We deliberately chose a two-bedroom unit, since we hoped to start a family soon. Life was wonderful, the fulfillment of our dreams, even though the cloud of deployment still hung over our heads. Dawn soon got a job at Char-Broil Grills, and we enjoyed getting to test out the new models as they came along. I'd assemble them in the middle of our living room floor, and then we'd put them to use out on our tiny deck only three feet wide, even if it was chilly January.

I soon realized that I had married an incredibly principled, moral young woman. I knew this from the past, but now I was seeing it on a daily basis. This connected with something that had happened in the spring with a close friend in the Ranger reconnaissance regiment, Kurt Smith. He and I were the same rank and hung out together a lot before Dawn arrived.

At one point he went home on leave—and returned radically changed. He had turned his life over to Jesus Christ, and it clearly showed. Right away his language changed for the better, his music choices cleaned up, and his general attitude brightened. He began telling others in the detachment about Christ and what a difference he had brought to his life. It was unmistakable.

I had to admit that although I had been a declared Christian for nearly a decade, my daily life didn't reflect it. I looked at the way Kurt acted and felt guilty.

Then I went home at night to Dawn and sensed more of the same. The two of them, without lecturing me in any way, were shining a spotlight on my inconsistencies. I was definitely rough around the edges, behaving pretty much the way most young enlisted men in the army behave. I would lie in bed at night and think, *God, I know I'm not matching up to these two at all.*

I decided this wasn't right, and I was going to clean up my act. Yes, the army atmosphere can be challenging for anyone who sets his mind to honor God. But since when did I shrink back from a challenge?

I began disciplining myself to speak without the usual splatter of four-letter words that are epidemic in army talk. I could get my point across just as well without them.

I decided I should also stop drinking. Alcohol had not been a problem in my life, even though I was raised in a beer-drinking family. Great-Grandpa Struecker, in fact, came to this country from Germany carrying the family recipe. His son got an official license to make beer in the state of Iowa. At every family gathering when I was growing up, drinking was just expected. I was handed a beer while still at the little kids' table for Thanksgiving dinner. Few of our family members ever grew irresponsible in their drinking, but it was definitely part of our culture.

The same held true now in the army. Almost every social event involved alcohol. Our reconnaissance detachment was small, fewer than twenty-five men, broken into three groups of seven, plus a couple of headquarters staff—and this only intensified the social connection. We seven guys did everything together. We went to the movies, we played volleyball, we hung out in each other's homes, our wives got together—and just about everything included a couple of beers.

But I had to admit that at this very time my mother was trying to overcome alcoholism. She struggled every time someone would put a drink in front of her. Was I going to be the one that caused her to give up the fight?

Kurt Smith never nagged me about this. Neither did Dawn. But I was hit by the apostle Paul's admonition: "Whether you eat or drink or whatever you do, do it all for the glory of God. Do not cause anyone to stumble" (1 Corinthians 10:31–32 NIV).

I'm going to quit, I said to myself. *It's no big deal. I can still hang out with the guys and have a good time. I'll just have a Coke instead of a beer.*

Well, it *was* a big deal to my friends. "Hey, what's wrong with you, Struecker?" they quickly asked. "How come drinking is bad all of a sudden? Come on!"

"I never said it was bad," I replied. "I just said I don't want to do it anymore. You don't have to do what I do. I've just made a personal decision here." I didn't want to get into a long discourse about the issue of alcohol. But they had trouble letting the subject drop.

I excused myself from going to see certain movies I would have seen in the past. Even more shocking in their view was when I started cleaning out my music collection. I had been born and raised on classic rock—Kiss, Van Halen, AC/DC, and the like. I had bought a lot of heavy metal as well, from Metallica to Megadeth. The lyrics started to bother me. No one ever preached to me about this subject, but the Holy Spirit silently began to convince me that this stuff wasn't healthy.

One day I got a big black garbage bag and began loading it up. By the time I was done, there were probably close to a thousand cassettes and CDs. I brought them into the unit, dropped them at the front desk where everyone checked in and out, and said, "Here you go—free for the taking. If you want any of this, it's yours." (Other people in my shoes would no doubt have thrown the bag in the Dumpster instead, but I didn't think of that.)

Shock waves went through the barracks. "What the *** is wrong with Struecker? He doesn't drink anymore, doesn't cuss anymore, now he's giving away all his music. He must have joined some cult!"

I wasn't swayed. I knew I was doing what was right, and the comments didn't bother me. I'd already heard what people said about Kurt Smith behind his back. When I told him about their ridicule, Kurt calmly said, "So? I'm not concerned about what they think." That became my stance as well.

Both of us knew that in the army culture, a lot of people look down on a soldier who's a Christian, thinking he's automatically weaker than the rest. He is assumed to be too compassionate and distracted with moral restrictions to be tough, that the enemy on the battlefield can exploit his weakness more easily.

I don't buy that point of view for an instant. As far as I'm concerned, the soldier with a moral foundation is stronger than the one without. The military likes to call itself "a band of brothers." Well, when you have the support of Jesus Christ, you have a friend who "sticks closer than a brother" (Proverbs 18:24 NIV). You have more stamina to endure difficulties and persecution.

I made it my goal to be the toughest, most competent soldier around—as a Christian. I would not be weak, but rather *meek*. The two words sound similar, but they're not. Meekness means having tremendous strength but intentionally placing it under the control of something else. I would develop my strength and place it under the control of Jesus Christ.

TOUGHER TESTS

The pace of Ranger life continued unabated, with frequent training missions in various locations. Dawn was left by herself in a strange environment with few friends, far from the familiar things of home. Then in December came another overseas deployment, which I describe in detail in the next chapter.

When I returned on December 12, 1991—having missed her birthday—she sat me down for a talk. "Do you realize," she said, "that we've been married nine months now, and you've been away from me for six of them? I mean, I knew the army was going to be a stretch, but this is crazy. I'm really tired of being by myself so much. Can you change to a different job or something?"

"Okay, I'll try," I said. "I promised you in the beginning that you were more important to me than my career. So let me see what I can do."

I immediately went to my commander in the reconnaissance detachment and said, "Hey, I think I'm ready for a different assignment. I want to go across the street to the Third Ranger Battalion and work as a squad leader. Think you could work that out for me?" Although still part of the Rangers, this position would involve less travel.

He wasn't wild about the idea at first, but by spring he had granted my request. I was assigned to Bravo Company and put in charge of a squad of nine men. The improvement in my schedule was quickly apparent. Dawn and I were happy about that.

This change did, however, put me in daily contact with a different breed of soldier. Whereas before I was part of a tight-knit group of specialists with strong personal goals, now I was handling very young, very immature guys who frolicked on the wild side whenever the chance came up. Their stories about what they did over the weekend were, if anything, more colorful than where I was before.

Every walk down the halls of the Third Ranger Battalion barracks was a trip through porno alley. Half a dozen TVs would be spewing different visual stimulation at the same time. It was hard to keep a clean mind, even for a married guy.

Among Rangers who were married, I observed that some viewed themselves as "geographical bachelors." When they were home at Fort Benning, they were faithful to their wives. But when they were elsewhere in the world, they felt entitled to do as they wanted. I'm sorry to say that some of their wives figured out the double standard and proceeded to act the same way while their husbands were away.

I sincerely wanted to influence this environment for good. I lived a consistent Christian life and made no attempts to cover up my faith. When my soldiers would use vulgar or profane language, I'd tell them I didn't appreciate it and not to use it around me in the future. After all, I was the staff sergeant in this squad and could set a certain standard.

Very soon I could tell that my life was being scrutinized on all sides. That was fine with me; I wanted to be a good representative of Christ. I was very much afraid of letting him down.

The subordinates in my unit never made a crack about me directly; they knew it would have been deadly to mock their sergeant. But if they were out of earshot, they would talk.

And meanwhile, my fellow noncommissioned officers (NCOs) spoke their minds freely. "Aw, don't even invite Struecker to go out with us," they sneered. "He's too busy reading his Bible." They sometimes accused me of preaching at them or judging them, even though I never told anyone on my level how he should live. All I said was, "Sorry, I personally don't drink" and that was called "preaching."

I wanted to say, "You know, you've never asked me what I really think about alcohol. You're just assuming that because I've stopped drinking, I'm condemning you. That's not the case at all."

The same dynamic was in play on the language issue, the music issue, and the adult entertainment issue.

I got weary of it at times. I knew I was in a better job for Dawn's sake, but the working conditions were harder. I found myself struggling to resist the ever-present temptations. I knew I wasn't a perfect Christian, and the thought of falling morally began to haunt me.

God, this is really tough, I prayed. *I don't know that I can keep handling all this pressure. How about getting me out of this?*

At times I wanted to leave the unit—and even the army. I know that sounds preposterous from a Ranger. But I was genuinely afraid of slipping up in one way or another. I didn't say anything to Dawn about this, but I brooded about it a lot.

We began to attend a nearby church, Fairview Baptist, on Sundays. I got to know several of the retired military men in the congregation, as well as others who worked in rough environments such as construction. Eventually I built enough of a friendship with several of them to reveal my struggle.

I'll never forget a couple of the older men saying, "Jeff, temptation is everywhere. You can leave the army, but it will find you somewhere else in another job. If you're a salesman on the road, the same pressures to compromise your marriage will be waiting for you. No matter where you go in life, you're going to have to stand tall in the strength that Christ gives. There's no running away from evil."

I really needed to hear that. I went back to read the well-known 1 Corinthians 10:13 again: "Remember that the temptations that come into your life are no different from what others experience. And God is faithful. He will keep the temptation from becoming so strong that you can't stand up against it. When you are tempted, he will show you a way out so that you will not give in to it."

I decided I might as well keep being a Christian in the Ranger Regiment. God needed men of character here, for sure.

The second thing that helped me was realizing that I would never be perfect or immune to these problems. The best I could do was to try to live differently and allow my example to influence other people. I couldn't get guys to change on my own. I could only be a conduit for the drawing power of God's love.

It became my agenda to show my unit and my peers that I could be as physically strong as anybody else, as mentally tough, as morally straight—and frankly, that as a Christian I could do even *better*. I began working harder than anybody else at comprehending military tactics. I began pushing my squad further every day to be physically fit. I used the occasional taunting to motivate me toward stronger, more effective leadership. The goal for me at the end of the day was to see if I could make guys say, "You know, if Jeff Struecker can be the kind of soldier he is and still be a Christian, then I guess Christianity is not for the weak after all."

I can't say how well I succeeded. That question will be answered only when I stand before God in heaven. But I do know that it served as a target for my personal life. It brought together the Ranger drive for excellence with the issues that matter most in life.

Members of 1st Ranger Battalion's Reconnaissance team before moving to the boarder of Kuwait and Iraq in late 1991. From right to left: Staff Sergeant Lowell McGee, Sergeant Corporal Palmer, Sergeant Joey Fink, and Captain Jeff Struecker.

Six

FOLLOW THE RULES

BY THE END OF 1991, MOST AMERICANS HAD PRETTY MUCH forgotten about Iraq. Our forces had put Saddam Hussein in his place in March, most of our soldiers and airmen had returned home from Desert Storm, and we were rightly proud of ourselves.

But Saddam had not forgotten about us. Seething in Baghdad over his humiliation, he decided to test the West and find out if we were still awake. He dispatched some twenty thousand of his remaining troops to the Kuwaiti border to see if anybody would notice.

We got the word in early December that the First Ranger Battalion, along with our reconnaissance detachment, would drop into Kuwait and put on a little show for the madman. The Kuwaiti government, of course, was more than happy to let us send a message to the watching Iraqi generals that if they dared step across the border again, things would get ugly right away.

I barely had time to grab my gear, rent a car, and hit the highway for the 250-mile drive across the state to Savannah, where the First Battalion planes would load up. But first this meant saying good-bye to Dawn for the first overseas mission of our married life. It was definitely hard.

"Honey, the unit just got orders. I have to go now."

"Where are you going?"

"I'm not allowed to say."

"When do you fly out?"

"Can't say that, either."

"How long will you be gone?"

"I don't know. Honest."

"When do you think you'll be back?"

"Don't know that."

"What is this mission all about? Is it dangerous?"

"Can't answer that. Just know that I really love you, and I'll get back to you as soon as I can."

I looked into her deep brown eyes and knew she was frustrated. So was I. This was all part of being a Ranger, but that didn't make either one of us feel any better. What a price to ask of a woman who had committed her whole life and future to me.

I knew she could take care of herself while I was gone. But that wasn't the point. I seriously did not want to be away from her. She was being asked to serve her country every bit as much by staying home alone as I was by going. It would be tough on both of us.

On the long flight across the Atlantic, I couldn't help thinking that this operation felt different from the previous ones. I was determined to do my job well as in the times before, but I had trouble getting away from my thoughts. *Hey, I've got a wife back there waiting now. I need to be a tad more careful this time, don't I? If I make a mistake out here, I'll be leaving a widow behind.* I mulled over the implications.

Large chunks of the flight time were spent in strategic planning.

We were told that our reconnaissance team would land in Kuwait City, transfer to other aircraft, and move to scope out a target site— a nondescript piece of desert right along the border. The First Ranger Battalion would follow several hours later, parachuting dramatically onto Ali Al Salem Air Base, a Kuwaiti facility. They would flash their equipment for the Arab-channel news cameras that would certainly be watching and then move out in our direction. For a couple of days they would unleash a show of thunderous firepower to say to the Iraqis: "If this is what you want, come on. We're ready for you!"

Another part of preparation in the air was the ROE (Rules of Engagement) briefing from a special-ops SJA (staff judge advocate— in other words, an army lawyer). "Here are the conditions for when you are allowed to engage an enemy target and when you're not," the officer stated. "Our goal here is not to start another war with Saddam. We're just serving notice to him that invading Kuwait again would not be a smart idea. However, if we come under attack from across the border, here is what you're allowed to do."

He then moved into a lengthy list of situations and rules, finally ending: "Anything else that doesn't fit what I've just covered, ask your commanding officer or NCO. He will make the decision on the ground."

The truth is, no army in the world wants to go into combat without rules. I'm aware that civilians sometimes think war is a case of "no rules." That's not true. Soldiers know all too well that in such a climate, unspeakable horrors would result—all the way from noncombatant injuries up to nuclear holocaust that annihilates everybody. No country wants that to happen.

Of course, outlining a set of logical rules in a classroom or on a transport plane is one thing; following them on the battlefield in "the fog of war," as it has aptly been termed, can be trickier. You think you've got it all straight in your head, but then things get complicated. ROE on paper—or on the little pocket cards they sometimes hand out—can appear to be thorough. All too often the real-world situation doesn't quite match up.

PINNED DOWN

I stepped off the plane in Kuwait City with a rucksack that must have weighed 120 pounds. Ammunition, a couple of MREs, a small field blanket, a toothbrush, and some toothpaste—plus thirteen quarts of water to sustain me in the desert and a punishing load of radio gear. I was hauling a satellite radio, satellite antenna, an encryption device, and a small team radio, complete with enough battery power to keep all of them running. And there were also my night-vision goggles and a spotter telescope.

Our reconnaissance team consisted of five guys plus a medic, Joey Fink, whom we of course hoped would have nothing to do on this mission. Just as we were ready to move out toward the border some thirty-nine miles from the air base, a nasty *shamal* moved in, a short but intense blast of rain, lightning, and thunder that happens occasionally in this part of the world. This forced us to travel by road instead. The terrain where we ended up was certainly not our favorite—just flat desert as far as the eye could see, with no hills or even trees to hide us from view. I did manage to find a small hollow maybe four or five feet lower than the rest of the desert floor. There Joey and I set up my radio gear.

We had met a Kuwaiti tank company along the way that had a

few U.S. Green Berets embedded with them. We exchanged a small amount of information and then proceeded to our objective.

Early the next morning, the other four members of our team split into pairs and fanned out in opposite directions to start gathering information for the battalion to come that night. From time to time, they would radio back to me what they were seeing, and I would compile it for transmittal to the First Battalion commander. This continued throughout the morning and into the afternoon.

All of a sudden, out of nowhere a single bullet flew over my head. *What was that?* I assumed it came from an Iraqi across the border only a hundred or so yards away. At least I could tell by the sound that the source was fairly close.

Joey and I immediately ducked. *Zing, zing!* came two more shots. I looked through my spotter scope to see if I could identify where the other two teams of our unit were. I couldn't see them.

The fire came more rhythmically now. Joey and I looked at each other. I gave him instructions on how we'd defend the communications gear if the worst unfolded and we got overrun by whoever was taking aim at us.

Just then the radio crackled to life. "Romeo Six Four, this is Romeo Six One," the code name of Sergeant Ulibarri, our team leader, who was out on the right flank with Staff Sergeant Lowell McGee.

"This is Romeo Six Four," I answered, trying to stay cool. "Go ahead."

"We're pinned down by enemy fire. Do we have authorization to return fire? Over!"

"Romeo Six One, stand by while I contact higher," I answered.

I began trying to get in touch with the commander of the First Ranger Battalion, even though I knew he was on the move by now and his radio guy might not be set up to hear me. I tried several times. I got nothing.

Sergeant Ulibarri was back in my ear, sounding more urgent this time. "Romeo Six Four, we're under direct enemy fire. Do we have authorization to fire back? Over!"

I told him I couldn't reach the local commander, so I was going to try for the Ranger base back at Fort Benning, using satellite.

I yelled at Joey to set up the antenna. "What direction?" he wanted to know, since radio communication was not his expertise as a medic.

"Just set it up, and I'll lock it in on the satellite," I answered. It took me a minute to dial in the correct frequency. The longer I worked, the more the incoming fire seemed to increase. I wondered what the four guys out there on level ground were doing to shield themselves.

I verified the azimuth and elevation to the satellite. Then I keyed the handset to check for receptivity. It took a couple of tries, but soon I got a strong signal.

"Romeo Base," I said, meaning the regimental commander or at least his staff, "this is Romeo Six Four. Over!"

A reply came back across thousands of miles. "This is Romeo Base, go ahead. Over." I could tell I was talking to some private with almost no experience.

At that moment, Sergeant Ulibarri broke through again, more agitated than ever. I asked him to stand by just a bit longer.

"Romeo Base, I've tried to reach the local commander, but he's en route, and I'm not able to reach him. We have a team that's pinned down under direct fire. Request permission to engage the enemy."

There was a long pause. I squirmed as more rounds flew over my head. This guy wouldn't have the authority to make the decision we needed.

I hated all this delay. "Romeo Base, this is Romeo Six Four. Over?" Minutes passed. I couldn't believe how long this was taking.

IDENTIFICATION, PLEASE

Finally a more seasoned voice came on to say, "Romeo Six Four, what is your location? Over." It sounded like either the deputy commanding officer or the executive officer of the Ranger Regiment. I couldn't place him in my mind, but I knew I was finally connected to somebody who could make a decision.

I quickly shot back our grid location, then added: "Romeo Base, be advised that I am not the element who's pinned down right now. My Six One element is being engaged. I'm in a communications site. The rest of the reconnaissance element is split up into two teams of two each, and one of those teams has rounds directly over their head. They're face down in the sand right now and can't move. Over!"

"Romeo Six Four," came the voice again, "can you positively identify the source of fire? Over."

I called Sergeant Ulibarri to ask.

"Hey, man, I can't even lift my head up without getting it shot off!" he yelled back.

Joey and I scanned the horizon for muzzle flashes, a glare off a metal gun barrel, or anything that would prove this fire was coming from the Iraqi side. We grabbed at any hint we could imagine. But I had to admit, "Romeo Base, the fire is definitely not coming from any known friendly force. However, I cannot 'positively identify' the source of fire. Over!"

The commander in Georgia was not impressed. "Romeo Six Four, get me the source of fire!" he demanded.

I passed this order along to Sergeant Ulibarri. "Roger!" he yelled, with rounds still flying over his head. He called the other recon element, the two men on the other side of the target, to see if they could shed light on the subject. We all knew the fire was coming from the Iraqis; we just couldn't prove it.

"Romeo Six Four, they can't identify," came the message. "But we're getting hammered. What does base want us to do?"

My heart ached at the words from my unit leader. "Romeo Base," I began saying once again, "we can determine the direction of fire, but we cannot determine who is pulling the trigger. Our recon team is getting hammered. Request permission to return fire! Over!"

"Romeo Six Four," came the steely voice on the other end, "you are *not*, I repeat *not* authorized to return fire unless you can positively identify the source of fire. Just hunker down and ride it out. I do not want an international incident here. Do you understand? Over."

I sank back onto the sand. "Romeo Base, I understand. Out."

How was I going to tell my boss, with bullets flying just inches over his head, that he and the others couldn't do a thing about it? I took a long breath, then clicked the transmit button again.

"Romeo Six One, this is Romeo Six Four," I said as slowly and compassionately as possible. "Romeo Base will *not* authorize you to return fire, for fear of an international incident. I'm sorry. I guess you're just going to have to put your head down and low-crawl back to this location. Over."

There was a pause. "Roger. Out." Sergeant Ulibarri's tone was flat, not revealing a tenth of the anger he felt, as well as the anxiety.

I was as frustrated as he was. "Stupid ROE," I muttered to myself. "Somebody's going to get killed over this. Don't those guys back in Georgia understand that?"

It was at least an hour before Ulibarri and McGee came slithering into our site. They were covered with sand from head to foot and completely exhausted. I could tell they were more than a little shaken by what they had just been through. Soon the other two guys showed up. Just about that time, the enemy fire began to slack off. We walked back from the border to meet up with the First Battalion, which was just arriving. As I walked, I thought, *Whoever that lone gunman is out there taking potshots at us is about to see one of the greatest displays of military might on earth.*

Sometime after midnight the First Battalion began its demonstration. For six hours or so, it pounded away from two angles at a target technically inside Kuwait, but well within view across the border. The impact of the show was bone rattling. The ultimate result was that Saddam got the message and began pulling his soldiers back from the border in less than twenty-four hours—which was the overall point of the mission in the first place.

My team and I left the Gulf just six days after we arrived. We felt as if we had lived a year in that length of time. Once I calmed down, I grudgingly admitted that the officer in Fort Benning made the right call that scary afternoon.

I learned again that my job as a soldier was to do my duty, even when I didn't like it and was seriously unhappy about the conditions. If I ever rose to command responsibility at any level, I would have to convince other soldiers to do this, too, without complicating the mission even more than it already was. Combat is difficult enough without somebody like me making up his own rules or deciding independently that a superior doesn't know what he's talking about.

Submitting to a higher authority is one of those life struggles that frustrates us all from time to time, both in and outside of the military. We fuss and gripe about how unrealistic the directive is. We long to be calling our own moves, instead of having to obey a superior, whether it's a colonel, an employer in an office, or God. Our independent spirit doesn't want to be tamed.

But compliance is necessary, and often turns out for our own personal good. In the heat of the moment, we don't see all the angles. The larger picture must not be forgotten.

I would need this perspective even more when I got to Somalia in just twenty more months.

The "Log-walk, Rope-drop" event over Victory Pond in the Best Ranger Competition, Fort Benning, Georgia.

Seven

Round Two

The conference auditorium at Fort Bragg, North Carolina, was jammed that hot August day in 1993—senior offi-cers in the front rows, junior officers behind them, and lowly ser-geants like me sitting on folding chairs against the back wall. We'd been gathered from far and wide (my unit had been called in the middle of a training mission in Texas) to hear what the United Nations wanted us to do in a hot, sandy corner of Africa called Somalia.

Represented in that room was not only our Third Ranger Battalion but also a number of other special operations groups. We were all lis-tening carefully to soak in information about the coming assignment.

The lights dimmed and the projection screen descended from the ceiling. Video footage of Mogadishu, shot from a low-flying helicopter, began to roll. The quality was incredibly good. The only trouble was, the picture moved so *fast* from one scene to the next. We all sat there thinking, *Slow down, man! I need to see that building a little longer.* The explanation was that "Mog," as the city was known among soldiers, was too dangerous for a U.S. helicopter to just hang out over the rocket-infested neighborhoods. If the crew wanted to stay alive, they had to keep moving briskly across the landscape.

Occasionally during the briefing, the speaker froze the video frame on certain critical landmarks. An NCO near the front who had recently spent six months in Somalia with the Tenth Mountain Division and had qualified to join the Ranger Regiment was able to add "color commentary" on this site and that intersection and the other marketplace. We were like a team of surgeons studying lab reports before heading into the operating room. The longer the intelligence portion of the meeting went on, the more confident I felt about making this mission work.

More than an hour passed by the time the lights came back up and a short stretch break was announced. Soon we were back in our seats for the ROE (Rules of Engagement) briefing, to be conducted by Staff Judge Advocate Gary Walsh.

"Okay, men, let me start by reminding you of the provisions of the Geneva Convention," he began, which was all old stuff to us. Next he reviewed the U.S. Military Code of Conduct—we could have quoted it to him from memory. Following that he spent another block of time on what could and could not be revealed by prisoners of war. Once again, the audience was silently thinking, *Yeah, yeah, we know.* The previous year I had been through the rigors of the army's SERE School (Survival, Evasion, Resistance, Escape), which included a grueling multiday simulation of captivity. *I have no intention of becoming a POW to some Somali warlord,* I said to myself.

Finally Gary got to the ROE for this mission—the part we had all been waiting for.

"This operation is different from what has happened in the past months," he explained. "That's why the UN has even given it a different name: UNOSOM II, which stands for United Nations Operation in Somalia Version Two, as opposed to UNOSOM I. The main goal is to stabilize and safeguard the distribution of food and other relief supplies, so people stop starving to death and stop running from—or getting kicked out of—their homes.

"Nobody is real thrilled about us using force to make this happen. But they do recognize that Aidid and the other bad guys have to feel some pressure. Here is what we're authorized to do."

He then moved into one technical scenario after another. I sat there trying to memorize every point. He got to a critical case that I knew my squad and I would be facing: "When dealing with crowds of people, some of whom may be armed while most are not, here is the rule: always try to control the situation without the use of lethal force. Begin by standing where you can be seen and simply motioning for the crowd to disperse. Reinforce this with short phrases in Swahili, such as *Hatari! Simama, njia imesungwa!* Danger! Stop, road closed!

"If that doesn't work, raise your weapon as if to shoot. This may succeed in convincing the crowd that it would be a good idea to break up.

"If they don't disperse, however, then you begin what is called 'progressive lethality.'" I had not heard the term before, so I listened all the more carefully. "That means you gradually increase the level of impact. First, you use things such as diversionary grenades, which don't actually hurt anybody but sure get their attention.

"If that doesn't work and you're still being threatened, you select whoever seems to be the most aggressive member of the crowd—the rabble-rouser—and you shoot him in the leg. This will have an immediate effect on the crowd psychology.

"You keep going with other leaders of the crowd if necessary. The lethality keeps rising to the point that the crowd finally breaks up.

"Let me add this very important point: under no circumstances do you shoot until you know that the target person is carrying a weapon. In fact, if possible, don't shoot until the weapon is pointed at you. Don't shoot to kill unless you absolutely have to; prisoners are always more valuable to us than bodies."

I sat there imagining how this was going to work. I already knew that my unit's job once we landed would be running the ground convoys on the outside of an objective's perimeter. Special operators would drop into an objective to capture the target personalities, and we'd been sitting out at the edge of things waiting to take the prisoners away. That meant we were the most likely to encounter large crowds of people who wanted to interrupt our efforts. We'd be the first barrier of protection for the assault soldiers inside the area.

What if we got overwhelmed? What if "progressive lethality" didn't work and the agitated crowd just kept coming? At that point, we would need backup from the skies. We'd need AC-130 Spectre gunships or air force A-10 Warthogs or some of the navy's F-15s to come roaring in and scatter the people—

What did I just hear? Gary Walsh was saying something about ". . . no air support on this mission. No collateral-damage munitions. The highest levels of our government are very concerned about escalating the force in Somalia. Nobody at the Pentagon wants to be remembered as the person who got us into 'another Vietnam.' We're going in with shooters to try to back off the warlords' militias, but that's all. Nothing that would wipe out whole blocks of the city and polarize the political environment."

He had to be kidding. I had trained my whole military career with aircraft flying overhead that could get me out of a jam if I were really in trouble. We were used to bringing enough firepower to wipe out anything and anyone who dared set foot in the way of our mission. We joked that we were the military equivalent of FedEx: "When it positively absolutely has to be destroyed overnight—send Rangers."

The frustration level in the room was thick. It broke loose as soon as Gary dared to ask, "Are there any questions?" Hands shot up all over the room. The NCO near the front who had already been to Somalia went first.

"Okay, what if there's a Somali on the street with an AK-47 looking right at me, but he's cleverly positioned himself right behind two women? Am I allowed to fire at him before he takes me out?"

Gary Walsh hesitated. "Well, I can't tell you what to do in every situation," he finally said. "You will have to decide." This only triggered more follow-up questions from the audience. He kept pausing before he responded.

"What if we're in a convoy moving along the road at forty miles an hour, and bullets start flying at us from behind some trees or bushes? We can't see the shooters, but we obviously know they're there. Are we allowed to fire back?"

"What if a roadside bomb goes off, and we're lucky enough to still be alive? Can we respond with force?"

"What if I'm in a helicopter and we're getting shot at from below?"

It soon became apparent that the "hard and fast" Rules of Engagement were not as comprehensive as they seemed. Somalia was going to be a dicey situation all around. Gary Walsh tried to tell us we had more flexibility than other forces. "You guys have no idea how long and hard my team and I fought to get rules even this lenient," he said. "You may not have all the latitude you want, but trust me—it could have been a lot tighter."

The Q&A time went on for a couple of hours, and by the time the meeting ended, everybody was buzzing. The hour was late. I walked back toward the balcony of a maintenance building where my unit was staying, trying to figure out how to present what I had just heard. How could I realistically prepare my men for this mission?

When I arrived, everybody was asleep except for my two team leaders, Danny Mitchell and Tim Moynihan. They had stayed up to wait for me. "Hey, what's up?" they asked when they saw me. "What did you find out?"

"Come over here, so we don't wake up the other guys," I said, pulling them aside. "It was quite a meeting."

I described the reconnaissance video as fully as I could. Then I went through the intelligence update. I talked about crowd control in general terms. Then I said, "Hey, it's late. Let's get some sleep. Tomorrow's going to be a busy day—and night."

"No, no, no," the two responded. "What's the full ROE? Come on, man—give us the scoop."

I took a deep breath and then unloaded the rest of what I had heard. I described "progressive lethality," and I informed them that we'd have no air support. "Listen, guys, I don't like this either," I admitted. "I was about to snap until I heard the one guy who'd already been in Somalia say they couldn't even return fire without getting authorization from higher up. It didn't matter if your buddy right next to you had just been killed. So at least we're better off than that.

"Here's the deal: when it's time to pull the trigger, pull it. Do the right thing, and I'll always back you up. I'll take any heat for what you do. I believe in you guys and know you'll make good decisions.

"Tomorrow I will summarize this for the rest of the squad. I'll basically tell them to watch the three of us and do what we do."

That night in my rack, I stayed awake praying for a while. I asked God to give me the ability to inspire confidence in my squad, despite the limitations. I prayed that he would help my words be clear and memorable. Eventually a little speech starting taking shape in my brain, and I fell asleep.

The next morning, I gathered the group around me. They all knew I'd been in an important meeting to outline this mission. "Guys," I said, "I talked with your team leaders after I got back last night. They now know what to do in any situation. When we get to Somalia, you just basically watch your team leader. Where he aims, you aim. When he shoots, you shoot.

"Don't do anything different than what you've ever done in the Ranger Regiment. Mitchell, Moynihan, and I will be using solid tracer rounds. You put your bullets where our tracer rounds are going, and everything will be just fine."

Stumbling Around

By 5:00 p.m. on Sunday, October 3, the guys had followed my instructions during the bloody run into Mogadishu and back out again, but things were definitely not going "fine." Dominick Pilla was already dead. Several dozen Rangers and others were still trapped. We were in a dogfight with a ferocious pack, and it was time to engage them once again in order to reach Mike Durant's downed Black Hawk.

Exactly where that helicopter was, nobody could quite tell me. I stood in the Joint Operations Center scrutinizing the satellite photo. "It's somewhere right in here," said Lieutenant Larry Moores, pointing to the area south of the Olympic Hotel that we called Shanty Town because it was jammed with masses of humanity that had come to Mogadishu for food.

"So, how am I actually going to find the bird, sir?" I asked.

"We'll just start out, and the guys up in the helicopter will give you directions as we go." That didn't sound foolproof to me, but what choice did we have?

A more immediate challenge was rounding up enough soldiers to go on this mission. All our best shooters were already in the city needing help. Who was left to rescue them? I still had my remaining eight guys, of course. We started grabbing support personnel—cooks, intelligence analysts, desk clerks—people who normally didn't go into combat. They were trained as Rangers, but they certainly hadn't faced the fire in a long time. *This group is going to be like the butcher, the baker, and the candlestick maker,* I thought.

We pulled out of the gate with my Humvee in front again, Lieutenant Moores's Humvee right behind me, then three five-ton trucks, and finally two more Humvees. I put my buddy Danny Mitchell at the rear, since he and I worked together so well. We could almost read each other's minds from a block away.

As we neared the K-4 Traffic Circle, the Black Hawk above told me, "Okay, now go down the main road running east, then turn left when I tell you." I did what they said, which put us onto a very narrow street, hardly more than an alley. We had gone about a hundred meters when I spotted a pile of burning tires ahead of us. This was the standard Somali signal to fight, as if to say, *Hey, everybody, over here! Bring your gun and come!*

I radioed to my eyes in the sky: "I've got burning tires in front of me." They knew what that meant as well as I did.

"Okay, take a right at the next chance," came the reply.

Before I could follow through, bullets began flying from the right side of the street, no more than ten feet away. "Action right!" I heard a Ranger scream in the Humvee behind me. We immediately began returning fire. Then out of the corner of my eye I saw a Somali getting ready to launch an RPG (rocket-propelled grenade). *Boom!* The rocket went screaming just a few feet in front of my face. It literally skipped off the hood of my Humvee like a rock on a lake and detonated into the concrete wall on the other side of the street. The impact lifted my vehicle up onto two wheels and threw it back down again.

The automatic-weapon fire coming our way was intense, just as it had been on the previous trip. Things in the city had not improved over the last hour—that was for sure. *I can't drive these cooks and intel guys through this,* I told myself. *It would be bad enough for seasoned infantrymen.*

"Back up!" I yelled to my driver. "Put it in reverse and step on it. They'll figure it out!"

He did as I ordered, slamming into Lieutenant Moores's vehicle. His driver got the idea and began backing up as well. We kept pushing, until gradually the whole convoy backed out of that narrow street. I kept looking around to see who had been hurt in the barrage. I feared to see the damage we had sustained.

Amazingly, I saw no blood. Nobody was crumpled down in pain. Everybody was up and firing at the enemy.

This was incredible! Every bit of hot lead thrown at us at such close range had missed. I couldn't believe it. I mean, Aidid's men may have been poorly trained shooters, but not *that* bad. I honestly had to give God credit for shielding my guys "in the valley of the shadow of death" (Psalm 23:4 NKJV).

I called the helicopter overhead and asked for a different route to the crash site.

"Okay. Just go around one block to the right," came the reply. "You can get there that way instead."

But that put us into an equally difficult problem. Straight ahead of us was a mound of dirt in the middle of the street, with everything from junk furniture to rolls of barbed wire piled on top. Should I just try to blast through it? No, that would not be a good idea, especially for the trucks behind me.

"That won't work, either," I called on the radio. "I need something else."

"Well, the only choice would be to go all the way back to the K-4 Circle, head north on Via Lenin, then cross over on 21 October Road, and approach the crash site from the opposite end of things. Are you sure you want to do that?"

"Better than getting blown up in this neighborhood," I answered. "We'll go for it."

I radioed back to Danny and the others about our latest plan. As we were driving, I paused a minute to marvel at the lack of strategy our enemy had evidenced in the first narrow street. Obviously no one had instructed them that if you're attacking a convoy, you let the first couple of vehicles pass by. You wait for the big trucks in the middle to come along. They're a bigger target—and if you stop them, you've effectively chopped the convoy into two parts, destroying its ability to function as a whole. Instead, these guys just unloaded their RPG at the first vehicle (mine), failed to take me out—and gave me the opportunity to escape.

Amid sporadic gunfire from both sides of the road, we arrived back at the K-4 Traffic Circle and swung around to head north.

Within a block or so, who should be coming our direction at that moment but Lieutenant Colonel Danny McKnight's group—the ones I left near the Olympic Hotel a couple of hours before when assigned to bring the injured Todd Blackburn back to base! They had been wandering back and forth in search of the first downed Black Hawk and getting beaten up all along the way. Now at last they were limping back to safety.

They were a tragic sight. One Humvee was so devastated it could no longer move on its own and was being pushed by another. We could see the arms and legs of dead soldiers hanging off the sides of vehicles. I didn't want to look at the faces of the Rangers who had lost their lives. It hit me hard when I saw the gray-skinned body of Sergeant Casey Joyce. He had worked for me as a team leader before recently being transferred to another platoon. There he sprawled, never to fight or smile or speak again.

"Stop!" Lieutenant Moores ordered our group, focusing on the wounded. "We need to help these guys. Get their casualties onto our vehicles so we can rush them back to the airfield. Take care of this situation first, and then we can go back out to find Durant's crash site."

Gunfire continued to crackle around us as we loaded wounded men onto our convoy. We also made sure to secure the captives inside the trucks, the sixty or more taken from the original target building. After all, they were the goal that had launched this whole operation.

We opted to leave the shot-up Humvee there on the road, rather than continue pushing it home. We needed to move as quickly as possible to save lives rather than equipment. Sergeant Aaron Weaver and I pulled out its radio and ammunition, then set off two thermite grenades that burn at about two thousand degrees Fahrenheit. One blew a hole in the engine block, the other in the center of the vehicle, rendering it useless to the enemy. Within minutes we were on the road back to base.

By now it was dusk. The sun was setting, darkness was coming quickly, and we were nowhere close to rescuing our men in the city. My second trip accomplished basically nothing, except to aid the return of McKnight's wounded Rangers. We still had a ton of work ahead of us.

Clearly Mohamed Farrah Aidid had many more fighters in Mogadishu than our surveillance had estimated. We should have engaged this battle with far greater force. Now we would have to find a way to regain the initiative, contain the damage, and get our guys out alive. But how?

Sky diving into a training mission while in the Ranger Reconnaissance Detachment.

Eight

THE ALL-NIGHTER

MAJOR CRAIG NIXON WAS THE SECOND SENIOR RANGER IN Somalia, and he came heading my way not long after we drove back into the airfield. I knew him from all the way back to Panama, where he had commanded a Ranger company, and I respected him greatly. "Jeff, you need to get the guys ready to go back out there again," he said. "We don't have everybody. In fact, it sounds like half the assault force is stuck at the first crash site, where Wolcott is. And nobody's made it to Durant's crash site yet."

"Yes, sir," I replied, not letting myself think about how ugly this effort was sure to become.

"This is the toughest thing I can ask of a bunch of soldiers," he added. "You guys already know how hot it is in there. It would be a lot easier if you *didn't* know what you were getting into. But you do. So make sure your men are ready for it."

Looking around, I asked, "How many guys do we still have?"

"I don't know—figure it out."

I knew I could count on some from McKnight's column that we'd just led back, although many of them were too wounded to help. Major Nixon broke into my thoughts to add: "The Tenth Mountain Division has already answered our call. And we're asking the UN to jump in with some of their heavy armor, too. The Pakistanis are going to help us out, and so are the Malaysians.

"So get us lined up, and we'll go to meet them up at the port, so we can put together a serious rescue convoy." With that, he turned away.

Two thoughts ran through my mind. One was practical: *As long as there are Rangers still out there in the city, my job's not over. I have a significant responsibility here.* The other was reflective: *I really am going to get killed tonight. I've made two runs already and lived to tell it—but now comes a third one. This is probably it for me.*

I was not distraught about the likelihood of dying. I actually felt calm inside. I believe God gave me that peace, an extension of knowing that I belonged to him, and my future was in his hands. My stomach didn't churn; I already had faced the facts about mortality and eternity. Based on that understanding, I turned to the task at hand.

"Rangers, over here!" I yelled. Some fifty soldiers gathered around me, while I stood up on a metal folding chair.

"All right, men, listen up," I began. "Here's what's going on. We've got a bunch of our guys pinned down at Wolcott's crash site. So far as we know, nobody's yet made it to Durant's crash site. The plan is now to put together a massive force—us, Tenth Mountain, and UN troops—to roll in there and rescue everybody.

"Yes, it's going to be complicated. We've never operated with some of these people before. The Pakistanis and the Malaysians even speak different languages. But we *have* to make this work.

"Everybody who's physically able, get your ammo and your

equipment so you're ready to go. We'll stand by until we're told to move over to the port."

The group was very quiet and somber. They knew, as I did, that we were headed into a deadly environment. But they also knew our friends in the city were counting on us.

The call to move out didn't come until around 9:30 that evening, by which time we were frustrated at the delay. On the radio we could hear our buddies calling for reinforcement or for medevacs to lift the wounded out. "Let's get moving!" we snapped more than once.

At the port two miles up the coast, the Pakistanis arrived with two American-made M-60 tanks, while the Malaysians brought twenty-eight armored personnel carriers (APCs), white with blue UN lettering on the sides. Altogether we had nearly a hundred vehicles, a fearsome collection of firepower. But still we waited, and waited some more.

We were especially worried about Corporal Jamie Smith, one of our best marksmen, who while trying to help secure the first crash site had taken a bullet in the thigh that had traveled up into his pelvis, piercing a femoral artery. Medics were frantically working to control the bleeding, but weren't making much headway. Smith was conscious and in agony. Urgent calls for a chopper to lift him out kept coming, and the air commanders replied that if another Black Hawk or even a small helicopter tried to land in that area, it would never come out again. Rescue would have to come on the ground, not from the sky.

Around ten o'clock came the news that Jamie Smith had bled to death. They simply could not keep pumping fluids into his arm fast enough to keep him alive. When I heard this, I was absolutely livid. "What in the world is taking so long?" I snarled to no one in particular. "We've got guys dying in there while we sit around getting organized and talking about coordination. This is ridiculous!" I felt utterly helpless.

FIREWORKS SHOW

It was 11:30 before we were finally lined up, a convoy stretching nearly two miles. It reminded me of a train hauling grain across the cornfields of Iowa. *This force would be as difficult to stop as that freight train*, I told myself.

I heard the command sergeant major of the Tenth Mountain Division tell his troops: "When we get into the city, shoot anything that moves. It's only bad guys out there now."

That wasn't true! I ran from vehicle to vehicle saying, "Hey, just a minute! We've still got Rangers in the city. So *don't* shoot anything that moves; make sure it's an enemy before you fire away."

As we rolled out of the port, the sporadic AK-47 fire was worth little notice. In two minutes, we reached National Street—one of the most identifiable boulevards in the city. It was one of only a handful of streets that could accommodate more than one vehicle at a time. Most of the others were too narrow to start with and were further cluttered with the charred remains of a hundred burning tires or the jagged metal skeletons of what once were vehicles. These had been destroyed by command-detonated mines placed in potholes, silently awaiting anyone dumb enough to drive over them.

In contrast, the traffic still flowed easily on National Street. This was also the dividing line of the city, an unseen boundary for the feuding warlords.

We turned left onto National, heading toward the Olympic Hotel and the original target building where Aidid's lieutenants had been captured. I watched in awe as the lead Pakistani M-60 tank turned the corner and immediately came under heavy fire. Next came the Malaysian APCs, and a barrage of gunfire pelted them. *How stupid can the enemy be?* I gasped. Trying to stop tanks and APCs with AK-47 rifles was about like throwing golf balls at a rhinoceros.

Regardless, I had to admit that any hope of intimidating our enemies with this massive show of force was unrealistic. Nothing was going to come easy this night. We were going to have to fight for every inch of ground as we moved to the two sites where our two Black Hawk helicopters had been shot down.

Our convoy answered the enemy fire on National Street with a display of small arms and rocket fire that was equal to any Fourth of July fireworks show. It was almost magnificent to watch that much lead flying back and forth right in front of my eyes—until I remembered that my squad's turn would come soon.

"Hunker down and get ready!" I radioed to Danny Mitchell on our other Humvee. We turned the corner and were immediately greeted with the same level of fire the tank and APCs had received. I offered up a simple prayer and then started to identify targets for Brad Paulson to engage with the .50 caliber machine gun on top of my vehicle.

The AK-47 fire ebbed and flowed all around us from that moment on as we exchanged punches with the Somalia militiamen. Every time we bloodied a nose, they blackened an eye. It was a tit-for-tat fight between two hundred U.S. special-operations soldiers and a city of people who had lived their entire lives with bullet holes in the walls and guns on the breakfast table. Every man in the city who was willing and able to pick up a weapon against us had already done so. By this point we realized that a lot of the people squeezing the triggers of those AK-47s were women and even some children. They had watched their fathers or brothers die just hours before and felt compelled to uphold the family honor. *I don't think I've ever known a country so willing to send all of its people to fight and die,* I thought.

I turned to my men and said, "Hey, conserve your ammo. We don't have enough ammunition to keep this up for hours and hours. Only shoot at what you know are bad guys. Besides, there are still Rangers in here."

About midnight we arrived at our destination near the intersection of National Street and Hawlwadig Road, within a few blocks of both crash sites. From there one set of troops began fighting toward the Wolcott location, while another headed for Durant. My men and I waited on the street to be called up to whichever spot needed more help. Meanwhile, gunfire, rocket-propelled grenades, and hand grenades kept coming our way without a pause.

Every minute the tension got a little higher, and the situation grew more deadly. The AK-47 fire became rhythmic; every three to five seconds a 7.62-millimeter round would pass overhead. Many of the rounds slammed into the wall next to us, while others passed within feet or even inches of our heads. Some, however, hit their intended targets. Brad Paulson, my young machine gunner up on top of the vehicle, got a graze wound across his forehead that began bleeding down into his eye. But he could still function.

I thought, *You know what? We're the easiest target in town. We're every rifleman's dream sitting here, and there's nothing I can do about it but keep fighting and praying.* In all my military past, I certainly had never been such a sweet enemy target. I was amazed we were still alive.

Simple guerrilla tactics should have been able to destroy every one of our vehicles and kill half the force without taking so much as one casualty. The sheer volume of men and women arrayed against us could have hit from a dark alley, run for cover, gotten more ammo, and hit again from a different direction. In this situation there was no way for us to defend against such tactics. But the Somalis didn't have this expertise. All they had was an unlimited supply of guns and rocket-propelled grenades.

Crack! Another AK-47 bullet snapped me back to reality. We returned fire every time we could pinpoint the enemy. The more we looked, the more we saw guns pointed at us from half the windows and doorways on National Street. As soon as we swung around to return fire in one direction, we got pounded from the other. Every time we got used to the rhythm of the AK-47 fire we would be hit again with another RPG. This continued all night long.

Sometime around two in the morning, a gunman up on a building right next to us kept peppering us with bullets. Brad Paulson yelled, "I see him up on the roof!"

"Okay—I've got a frag grenade here," I answered. "Throw it up there. That'll stop him good—but you have to cook it off, you know?" I handed the explosive up to Brad. "Don't throw it too soon, or else he'll have time to pick it up and heave it right back down at us. Here you go. The safety's still on."

Brad reached down and took the fragmentation grenade. He looked at it in his hand and then looked back at me. He looked down at the grenade again, still not doing anything.

I studied his boyish face and his skinny frame, which couldn't have weighed more than about 120 pounds. Suddenly I realized why he was hesitating. "You've never thrown a hand grenade, have you?" I asked.

He dropped his eyes and replied, "No, Sergeant."

"What happened in basic training, man? Everybody does this back at the beginning!"

He paused again.

"Were you on KP that day? Were you cleaning pots and pans in the chow hall while everybody else was learning how to throw a hand grenade?"

"Yes, Sergeant, I was."

I smiled. I could do it myself, of course, but I could also give him a lesson right here in the middle of the night. "Okay, you need to learn!" I said, teasing him. "First step is, we take the safety off. Then I'll pull the pin out. Next I'll pull the spoon off—and then I'm going to hand it to you, and you hold it until I tell you to throw it. Don't you dare throw it one second early!"

"Yes, Sergeant."

"And one more thing—you *better* get it up on the rooftop, too!"

I went through the routine, handed it to him, then counted, "One! Two! Three! Now, throw it!" He flung it accurately up onto the roof of the building, where it detonated almost immediately—the first grenade toss of his life.

We never heard another peep from that rooftop the rest of the night.

WAITING, WAITING . . .

The Somali militia fighters kept firing from other angles, however. At one point a Humvee behind me was destroyed by a withering barrage. One guy was hit in the hand, while another took RPG shrapnel in the forehead. We pulled the casualties off to another vehicle so medics could try to patch them up.

I had some food in my pack, but I certainly wasn't going to pull it out in front of everybody else. Besides that, I could not afford to divert attention from the enemy even for a few seconds. I did manage to take one swig of water out of my canteen, but that was it.

The longer we stayed on the street, the more concerned I became. I looked at my watch. It read 4:40. We kept waiting anxiously to hear one word from our commanders over the radio: *exfil*—shorthand for *exfiltrate*, the opposite of *infiltrate*. That would mean all our casualties had been collected and all of the bodies were accounted for. Once that word was sounded, we could mount up and get out of this dreadful place.

But it didn't come.

An RPG went off right next to my Humvee with a thunderous boom. Brad Paulson came falling down into the vehicle from his post up on top, clutching his right hand and screaming, "*Aaaaaggh!*"

Steaming hot shrapnel had burned through most of his hand. I could hear the sizzle of flesh. I whipped out my canteen and starting pouring water on his hand to douse the torture. He gasped for air and then grew quiet.

"Are you okay? Can you move your hand?" I asked, holding it in my own.

"I can't move my fingers. But I'm all right," he insisted.

We both looked down. The metacarpal area was as red as a chili pepper. I took out a bandage and wrapped it up. He seemed to get his bearings once again.

"Okay, man, just grab a seat in the back," I instructed. "I'll put Moynihan up there on the machine gun in your place. Or I'll do it myself. You take a break."

In that moment, the character of a Ranger came rising up. "No, Sergeant," Paulson replied. "It's my gun. I'll take it."

"Dude, what are you talking about? You can't even use your right hand now. It takes a lot of strength to work a .50 cal."

"I'm okay," he insisted. "I'll stay on the gun." He got up to resume his post, refusing to quit.

I argued with him some more. I told him he'd already been up there for hours. I had no problem with him taking a break now. He wouldn't listen to me.

Soon he was back atop the Humvee, aiming at targets and firing away left-handed. When it was time for a new ammo can, one of us would hand it up to him. He would place it in position, insert the feeder and then proceed to charge the gun, even though this is definitely a two-hand operation. Brad somehow figured out how to accomplish the task using his left hand and his right forearm.

I let him keep firing for a while and then again tried to relieve him. "Seriously, man, I'll put Moynihan on the gun. You're fine—don't worry about it."

"Hey, Sergeant, it's my responsibility. I'll stay on it," he insisted.

I sat there in the Humvee thinking, *This kid's only about nineteen. What was he doing a year ago right now? Probably going to his high-school homecoming game. Here he is tonight, and I've already made him wash blood out of the back of a Humvee—now he's got a chunk taken out of his forehead and then burning shrapnel on his hand—and he won't quit.*

Where do you find guys like this?

LEAVE NO MAN BEHIND

At last the sun's rays began to brighten the eastern sky. This close to the equator, the sun rises and sets much more quickly than at northern or southern latitudes. It seems as if you switch from total darkness to full daylight in about fifteen minutes.

Every passing minute we could see more of our surroundings—and our enemies could see more of us. The gunfire got more and more intense. I radioed for help. "Can you give me a helicopter to do a gun run down this road?" I asked.

"Can't help you," came the reply.

Then, however, a voice from the Tenth Mountain group spoke up. "We can send you an Apache." Soon this fearsome gunship came screaming overhead and sprayed one entire side of the road. That shut the enemy up for a while, at least on that side.

Around 5:30 we could tell our vigil was nearing its end when some of the Malaysian APCs began rolling by our position. I sucked in my breath when I saw dead Rangers on top, their blood streaking down the sides of the white vehicles. Why were the bodies out in the open like that? Within seconds I figured out that the insides of the APCs must be full of wounded Rangers, so that those already dead had to be stashed on top like so many sacks of potatoes.

I strained my eyes to recognize the face of one body dangling off the top of the last APC, his head and one arm hanging over the side. Blood was smeared all along the white sheet metal below him. I couldn't make out the identity, except that he was definitely a Ranger. I watched in stunned silence.

Lieutenant Larry Moores called me just then in a clear, concise voice over the speaker box. "Romeo Three One, this is Romeo Three Six." I anticipated that this might be the long-awaited order to move out.

"This is Romeo Three One. Go ahead, over," I answered as calmly as I could.

"Three One, we are waiting for the last element to be pulled off the crash site before we extract. When we get the word, your two vehicles will take the extreme rear of the convoy. You have responsibility for rear security. Over," he said.

I fell back in my seat, deflated. We *still* were not ready to exfiltrate?

"Romeo Three Six, what is the holdup?" I asked calmly, but letting him know my dissatisfaction.

"Three One, this is Three Six. The crash site is pretty bad. They're trying to get the pilot's body out of the aircraft, but he's pinned in the wreckage. They have all the other bodies. They've tried to dismantle the aircraft to get him out, but it's not working. They're having to pull the body apart—" There was a long pause. "He should be out in the next ten to fifteen minutes."

The grisly picture in my mind left me without words. Why had I even asked the question? I regretted having this conversation on the speaker box. It would have been better to shield my squad from hearing it.

Leave no man behind. This was the army dogma in action. It didn't make pragmatic sense at the moment to keep the rest of us waiting in harm's way. But it was part of our commitment to one another, a declaration that every soldier was valuable and to be treated with dignity, whether alive or dead. We were a unit, and we would not abandon our fellow soldiers, no matter how great the personal hazard.

"Roger," I sent back to Lieutenant Moores. I looked away from my men. Nobody offered another comment. They knew as I did that to be abandoned is one of the worst things that can happen to a human being. With all the other suffering that we had sustained on this mission, we would not inflict that pain on anyone. We were a team, and we would win or lose together.

"Paulson!" I said, getting back to our immediate situation. "We're going to take up the rear of the convoy. When the last vehicle drives by, I want you to point that .50 cal down the road behind us. Anything that looks like a military target is yours to engage, since all the assault force will be ahead of us."

"Roger, Sergeant."

And then over the radio came the words we were all waiting to hear: "Prepare to exfil!" A charge of excitement filled the air. The collective sigh of relief was almost tangible. I told Private First Class Kerr, my driver, to turn the vehicle around and position it so we would be ready to move when the call came.

"Romeo Three One, this is Romeo Three Six." Lieutenant Moores was back on the radio. "You will be the extreme tail of this convoy. A couple more vehicles will roll by you. When you see the last tank roll past you, then you will know that the entire convoy is ready to move."

Why on earth is a tank going ahead of me? I thought. *Why isn't it going to be the rear of the convoy? Who's protecting who here?*

"Roger. Is Mitchell going to fall back, too, and wait for us when we get the word to move?" I asked, referring to my trusted team leader, Danny.

"Negative. He will stay with the lead element. You and I will be the last vehicles to leave."

"Hooah" was all the reply I could muster—the classic army reply for *I understand, sir,* even if I wasn't thrilled about it. It was the only word in my vocabulary that fit this situation.

Soon the thunder of the final tank approached. The ground began to shake beneath me, and my heart began to race. I had never been this close to a tank in motion before. I wondered if the driver saw us out of his porthole. I certainly hoped so.

"Kerr, put it in gear and hold your foot on the brake, just in case we have to get out of this guy's way in a hurry," I ordered. I didn't want to take any chances.

Whoooosh—boom! An RPG from behind us slammed into the tank's heavy armor, exploding off to the side. The next thing I heard was the whine of the tank's turret as the operator turned the main gun around. By then Paulson was already facing the rear as well, looking for targets.

The tank came within a dozen feet of us, and then *booooooooom!* went the response. I lost consciousness for a few seconds. The blast stunned us all. I didn't know up from down for a few seconds.

When my vision cleared, I looked back down the road and saw the whole side of a concrete building missing. Meanwhile the tank picked up speed and headed on toward National Street.

The sun kept rising over the fractured buildings. In spite of the blue tint in the air, I began to see the marks of war on walls and vehicles. I saw how weary my men looked from this operation. I hoped I didn't look as weary to them. This night had taken just about everything we had to give. But we were in the home stretch now.

Kerr kept his eyes on Lieutenant Moores's vehicle ahead. Slowly it pulled out from its position, with us right behind.

We had covered maybe a mile when Brad Paulson's voice came yelling from up above. "Sergeant! We've got bodies chasing after us from down the street!"

"Open fire," I ordered, assuming these were the Somalis who had fired the RPG at the tank just minutes before. "How many are there?"

"Looks like about ten."

"Open fire!" I shouted again. The enemy shots were becoming intense again, a constant snap of rounds going over our heads and hitting the walls right next to us.

But Paulson didn't fire. "Sergeant, I think these are our guys!" he yelled.

What? I exclaimed to myself. *There aren't supposed to be any good guys behind us. Didn't we get the word that all elements were accounted for before we heard the order to exfil? Yes. This doesn't make sense.*

I turned around in my seat and leaned my head out the window. I could not believe my eyes. There down the road, a dozen Rangers were running toward us and firing in every direction. I could see the look of terror with each step they took. They were watching us— their only hope for escape—go speeding away from them, and they were panicked.

"Romeo Three Six!" I called to Lieutenant Moores on the radio. "We've got bodies chasing after us! They look like our guys!"

He was not listening. With only one radio trying to keep up with three channels at once, he must have been talking to somebody else.

"Romeo Three Six!" I shouted again.

I turned to my driver. "Kerr, step on it! Get us up to the PL [platoon leader]!" I said, as Paulson began to engage Somalis that were firing at the men running up the road. Kerr floored the accelerator, and we caught up within seconds.

"Lieutenant Moores!" I screamed, not knowing if his window was up or down. "We've got some of our guys running behind us on foot! We have to go back and get them!"

"*What?*" his gunner called from up on top.

"Paulson, tell them to stop! Tell Moores we have good guys back there that are on foot running after us!" Paulson passed the word over to the other gunner, which got results.

All the preceding vehicles of our convoy had sped away from us, leaving us isolated in the street. By this time the Somali rate of fire was as thick as we had experienced.

"We have to go back for them!" Lieutenant Moores called from his vehicle. "Put it in reverse!"

From my rear view window I could see the guys on foot shooting everything they had in every direction. I looked at the remaining ammunition in my vehicle and began wondering if we would be left without a bullet to shoot before this was over. But we had to do what our comrades needed.

Kerr stepped on the gas, rubbing the side of Moores's vehicle and breaking off our rear view mirror. It would do him no good to look back through the Humvee, due to the bomb plate that separated the hatch compartment from the front. He was forced to drive blind. I tried to give him directions, but we drifted off the main road and ran into a fallen light pole. "Just keep on driving!" I yelled. *They sure don't teach you to do this in defensive driving school*, I thought as we sped back up the road.

"Slow down," Paulson said momentarily to Kerr. Then: "Okay, stop!"

Wide-eyed and exhausted Rangers as well as other special-ops soldiers began piling onto both vehicles—more than I could easily count. I saw the Humvee's back hatch spilling over with arms and legs of guys who just got partway on. The last man had obviously made a quick decision and leaped into the laps of his friends. His arms strained to reach the pant legs of the rest of the men in the vehicle. He buried his head and shoulders between the legs of other guys, and the rest of his body dangled like a noodle over the rear of the vehicle, his feet no doubt dragging the ground as we took off.

I reached over to slap Kerr's leg and yelled, "What are you doing, man? Get this thing moving!" We were poking along at less than ten miles an hour, it seemed.

"I've got it on the floor, Sergeant!" he hollered back. "It won't go any faster. We've just got too much weight in here!"

(By the way, the *Black Hawk Down* movie takes liberty at this point, showing the guys *running* all the way back to safety at the nearest UN-controlled facility, a soccer stadium. It makes a nice visual for the film—but that's not what actually happened. I know— I was there. They instead jumped onto our two Humvees and hung on for the ride back.)

The sun squinted across the morning sky as we lumbered down National Street. The pavement was littered with empty shell casings from all the bullets fired that night. I'd seen plenty of empty ammunition lying around training areas, but this was unbelievable. The streets glistened with golden sunlight from the brass casings. They filled so much of the street that it looked like the yellow brick road from *The Wizard of Oz*.

We had fought against an enemy far more numerous than us, on streets and alleys they knew far better than we did. We had suffered a heavy toll of pain and death. But we had fought honorably to the end, refusing to bail out on the mission or to compromise our pledge to our fellow soldiers. At last we could leave the field of battle with nothing to be ashamed of.

Prayer during Operation Enduring Freedom just hours after an enemy rocket attack in Afghanistan

Nine

SURVIVORS

AFTER THE GHASTLY NIGHT WE HAD ENDURED, RUMBLING into the shelter of the soccer stadium was like stepping onto a whole new planet. The morning sun was shining, the sky was blue, and for the first time in hours, none of us was getting shot at. A different kind of battle was now under way—a battle for the lives of dreadfully wounded men.

Off to one side, an orderly row of body bags was already getting longer and longer. Out on the turf, doctors and medics hovered over dozens of stretchers, hooking up IVs and bandaging wounds. They cut off the dirty uniforms to get to the gunshot holes and broken bones. The scene became more and more gory as the full extent of human damage was exposed to view. We knew without asking that a number of our friends were on the brink of death.

The loudest sound was the chop of helicopter rotors. One by one they airlifted casualties toward the field hospital back at the air base. It reminded me of that intro to the old television show M*A*S*H, where the air seems thick with choppers.

Those of us who emerged unscathed stood not quite knowing what to do with ourselves. We tried to figure out who was missing, how many we had lost, and who was in grave danger. In the midst of this, the Pakistani troops, who were using this stadium as their base, came around with trays of water in small glass cups. I took one and stared at it. *How in the world could there be an unbroken glass cup in all of Mogadishu?* I wondered.

Next one of the Pakistanis handed me a plate with some rice. I thanked him and ate a couple of bites, my first morsel of food since lunch the previous day. But my stomach let me know it wasn't interested. I drank the rest of the water and then retreated to my Humvee, noticing for the first time how many bullet holes it had. They were everywhere. Three of the four tires had been shot flat. No wonder we had poked along so slowly trying to get to this place.

I hopped up onto the hood of the Humvee and sat motionless. I watched my guys hugging each other and dabbing tears out of their eyes. Every so often, an officer would walk by and ask, "Hey, Jeff, did you know that so-and-so just died?" Strong men put their faces down between their knees and wept.

Different people react in different ways to pressure and its aftermath. While others mourned or tried to cover their emotions by talking or smoking, my reaction was subdued. I stared out at the scene before me, feeling numb. I didn't have words for this moment, and so I kept quiet. In fact I almost began to worry about my state. Why wasn't I emotionally affected like the guys around me? I didn't know the answer.

I was pulled out of my reflection by the order to drive our vehicles back to the airfield. Most of the casualties had been airlifted away, along with a number of healthy troops.

"We head back on flat tires?" I asked.

"Well, we don't have any spares here," Lieutenant Moores said, "but we're definitely not going to leave the vehicles behind. So you guys just figure it out."

It was a long grind of several miles driving on rims around the edge of the city, but eventually we made it home to the base. When we pulled through the gate, we met a scene of utter destruction. Shot-up helicopters were everywhere. Some vehicles were absolutely destroyed. They were leaking fuel onto the ground. To one side an engine was on fire, and soldiers were hosing it down.

Once again medical triage was at the center of attention. Doctors were battling fervently to stop the bleeding and control shock reactions. Three of the men most horribly hurt had already been flown out toward the large army hospital in Weisbaden, Germany. We heard that one had died soon after takeoff.

Captain Mike Steele, the Ranger commander who had fought through the night near the Wolcott crash site, was shocked when a sergeant handed him a list of those known to be dead—thirteen in all. Plus, six others from the Durant crash site were still missing, which he thought probably meant they were dead. The list of the injured came to seventy-three. Steele promptly walked toward the field hospital to start visiting them one by one, laying a hand on their shoulders and telling them he was proud of them.

Of my ten-man squad, I had lost Pilla the afternoon before—and that was all. Paulson and Specialist Bonnett, the other top gunner on Danny Mitchell's vehicle, were both wounded, but would survive. The remaining seven of us were intact. I quickly realized this was something close to a miracle, as I calculated how badly other units had been decimated.

Guys began clustering around TV sets, where CNN was showing live coverage from inside the city. "Somalis are rejoicing today over the downing of two U.S. helicopters . . . ," the news anchor said. And on the screen we saw people jumping up and down on top of the Black Hawk shells. We grimaced at jubilant crowds dragging bodies of American soldiers through the streets. We leaned forward and strained our eyes for clues—uniform patches, personal tattoos—anything that would tell us which of our comrades' bodies were being abused.

"That guy's an aviator!" someone said.

The picture soon changed. "Looks like a special operator," somebody else said, "but I can't see his face . . ."

The worst was when CNN began showing Somalis jamming bayonets into already dead soldiers. We were infuriated. War is violent, but this crossed the line into insult and savagery. When a man was already killed, they didn't need to desecrate his remains that way. And CNN didn't need to be showing it to the whole world. A flurry of curses rose up from the soldiers around the TV sets. We vowed to get those six bodies back whatever it took.

WHAT NOW?

I walked back to my cot in the hangar to wait until new orders came. I sat down wearily. I had assumed the night before that I would probably never return to this spot—but here I was. My life had been spared once again.

"Hey, Jeff," a voice said. I looked up to see one of my men. "I've got questions. I need to talk to somebody."

"Sit down here with me, man," I said.

"So, like—how could this happen? I thought we were supposed to be the best in the world."

"Yeah. Don't forget—we captured the two guys we were sent to get. But it sure cost us a lot, didn't it?"

We talked a little longer, just letting out the emotions. As soon as one guy stood up to leave, another stopped by. Throughout that afternoon and evening, and even the next morning, I found myself talking to one individual after another. They all knew I had declared myself to be a Christian, and they brought me their deep questions.

"Jeff, why would God let this happen?" some of them snapped. "If he had wanted to keep us from getting hammered so bad, he could have done it." They were genuinely angry and hostile at God.

I did not try to talk them out of their strong feelings. I just let them vent. Far greater minds than mine have struggled with why pain and suffering are so rampant in our world and how much of it is humanity's own fault.

Another line of questions rose not out of anger as much as apprehension about eternity. "What I want to know is, where's Pilla now? What's happened to him? And what's going to happen to me if I get sent out there to find those six bodies, and I get blown up? Then what?"

Earlier in my life, I might have put on a professional face and just said: "Hey, man, you're a Ranger! Don't get bogged down in all that stuff. Just suck it up and do your job." But now I tried to be much more personal. I sat quietly on my cot and gave them time to choke out their questions. Then I said, "I guess I didn't know Dom Pilla or Jamie Smith well enough to give a firm answer about where they've gone. What I do know is what the Bible says about all this: 'It is destined that each person dies only once and after that comes judgment' [Hebrews 9:27].

If a guy has put his faith and trust in Jesus Christ, he goes to heaven. If not—unfortunately, he doesn't. I wish I could tell you otherwise. But I don't make the rules, you know? I'm just trying to give you the Bible answer to your question."

I could tell that guys who had previously thought they were ten feet tall and bulletproof were now dealing with their own mortality. They were facing some of the heaviest questions of life. It appeared to be the first time for some of them. They weren't like me, having wrestled with this as a grade-school kid having nightmares back in Iowa. Instead, they had gone through a living nightmare on the streets of Mogadishu and were now facing the hard facts about this life and the next.

This led to follow-up questions about how to be sure of heaven. I would reply, "No amount of being a good person can get you into God's favor. A lot of people want to think that way, but it's not true.

"Jesus is the only one good enough to deserve heaven. And he made it possible for us to 'ride his coattails,' so to speak, if we'll turn from our sins and ask him to take us on. That's the amazing offer of grace that he extends to us."

This led to more discussion with a number of guys. I eventually got around to the point of decision: "Are you ready to commit your life to Christ?"

Some replied, "Well, I'd have to think about that some more." But at least a couple of guys answered, "Yes, I am." Right there on my cot, we bowed our heads and prayed together, asking God to forgive them and accept them into his family for now and eternity. They stood up knowing that if this coming night turned out to be their last night on earth, they would die knowing their ultimate destination.

I didn't pressure anybody. I just sat there on one end of my cot and let them come to me. Sergeant First Class Kurt Smith, my Christian friend since before I got married, was sitting on the other end doing the same thing with his own line of guys. At one point I looked off across the hangar and saw the chaplain with still another group of guys around him. Rangers were dealing with issues they needed to face.

In these moments, a small seed was planted in my mind about my personal future. Maybe I was meant to do more in the army than kicking in doors and throwing hot lead at the enemy. What if I prepared myself to focus on the spiritual readiness and strength of our regiment? That would obviously mean going back to school, and I saw no clear way to do that. But I was intrigued with the possibility of edging into some kind of ministry role.

I told myself that as an eighteen-year-old I had wanted to go to war and see how I would perform while being shot at. Well, I could now certainly put a check mark beside that one. I definitely had that goal out of the way. Was there a new goal for me? Should my career in the military take a different path from here on?

Not that I was all that intense about my spiritual life before coming to Somalia. Dawn and I had been going to a Southern Baptist church we liked for the past six or nine months, but we hadn't been totally committed to it. Neither one of us joined the church, for example. That was certainly going to change if I made it back home, I told myself. I wanted to be the strongest Christian I could be, and if God could make use of me in some kind of ministry down the road, I would definitely say yes. He had my full attention as a result of this ordeal.

SURVIVORS

Around nine o'clock that Monday night, October 4, everybody at the airfield compound who could still walk was called to a mass formation. General Wayne A. Downing, commander of all the U.S.

special operations across all branches of the military, had just landed straight from Washington. He had literally jumped on a Lear jet and whipped across ten time zones to be with us.

We lined up in front of the hangar: the Rangers in one set of rows, the aviators in another, and the special operators in another. I looked at our Bravo Company, which just a day before had been around 140 people—and there were hardly fifty of us still standing. The rest were either dead or lying in the hospital or on an airplane headed for Germany. I was sobered by the visual reality of how much we'd lost.

I looked down the row of my squad. Everybody was there except Pilla. *Man, I've got the biggest squad out here,* I said to myself in amazement. *I've got more people alive than that whole platoon right next to us.*

"You guys are terrific," General Downing assured us. "This battle will be remembered as the turning point. You've put Somalia on a whole new track. And you've upheld the special-operations tradition. I'm proud of every one of you." He went on with a full pep talk that I tried to believe, even though the pain of our losses was still fresh. I could only hope his prediction was true and this pathetic land would be better for what we endured.

Soldiers take a break to listen to the Word of God at Fort Irwin, California.

Ten

SLAP IN THE FACE

THE SITUATION AT OUR AIRFIELD COMPOUND HAD dramatically changed by Wednesday of that week. Huge C-5 cargo planes began landing about every thirty minutes, disgorging massive amounts of fresh equipment as well as troop reinforcements. The whole Alpha Company of the Third Ranger Battalion showed up—150 men ready and itching to help regain our momentum. A special-operations group arrived as well. The place fairly bristled with M1A1 tanks and Bradley Fighting Vehicles. A dozen brand-new Humvees came rolling out, with zero miles on their odometers. An entire package of assault helicopters and their crews landed from Fort Campbell, Kentucky.

Any Mogadishu resident watching the skies and listening to the thunder of incoming aircraft would have known that Washington was loading up for a big-time response. Aidid's street fighters may have beaten us up for one night, but payday was obviously coming soon.

Along with all the hardware and new personnel, a well-respected diplomat named Robert Oakley arrived Friday to make the point verbally. He had been the U.S. ambassador to Somalia when there was a functioning government, and his contacts were still in good order. He quickly set about to chat with Aidid's representatives, saying in essence, "You know, I've just talked with President Clinton, and it would probably be a good idea for you to return the six missing bodies right away—that is, if you want to keep your city from being totally blown off the map."

The cagey Aidid was in hiding, of course. He replied through his intermediaries with a trade offer: how about the bodies in exchange for the sixty or seventy captives the United States took in the Sunday afternoon raid? He felt that would be a reasonable swap.

Ambassador Oakley's reply was blunt: "No, no deal, no trade, no bargaining. You must give back the bodies *now*, or the full fury of the U.S. military will fall on your head without restraint. Fresh troops are already here and ready, and the engines are idling . . ."

The first body was quickly dropped off at our front gate. Several hours later, here came another one. The next day, another one. It was a miserable job to pull them inside the compound and take them to the medics for identification and preparation to fly home. We saw up close how brutally some of our comrades had been mutilated, and we gritted our teeth in disgust.

Some of the bodies had already been buried in shallow graves in the sand and then dug up again. One of the corpses showed up without a head. Robert Oakley went back to his contacts to say, "No, that's not good enough. You have to give us the head, too." The next day, the head was delivered to the gate.

Some of the bodies were so battered they could not be identified until they reached Dover Air Force Base in Delaware, where dental records and other information were available. Only then could families be given the awful news that their MIA (missing in action) loved one was KIA (killed in action).

During this time, Major General William Garrison pulled us together in front of the Joint Operations Center for a memorial service. This tough, rangy Texan spoke solemnly and sincerely about the good men we had lost in pursuit of our assigned mission. He used a modern adaptation of the famous St. Crispian's Day speech from *Henry V*, where Shakespeare put these immortal words in the mouth of the king trying to rally his outnumbered troops against the French:

> He which hath no stomach to this fight,
> Let him depart; his passport shall be made,
> And [coins] for convoy put into his purse:
> We would not die in that man's company
> That fears his fellowship to die with us.
> This day is call'd the feast of Crispian:
> He that outlives this day, and comes safe home,
> Will stand a tip-toe when this day is nam'd,
> And rouse him at the name of Crispian.
> He that shall live this day, and see old age,
> Will yearly on the vigil feast his neighbours,
> And say, 'To-morrow is Saint Crispian':
> Then will he strip his sleeve and show his scars,
> And say, 'These wounds I had on Crispin's day.'
> Old men forget: yet all shall be forgot,
> But he'll remember with advantages
> What feats he did that day. . . .
> This story shall the good man teach his son;
> And Crispin Crispian shall ne'er go by,

From this day to the ending of the world,

But we in it shall be remembered;

We few, we happy few, we band of brother;

For he to-day that sheds his blood with me

Shall be my brother; be he ne'er so vile

This day shall gentle his condition:

And gentlemen in England, now a-bed

Shall think themselves accurs'd they were not here,

And hold their manhoods cheap whiles any speaks

That fought with us upon Saint Crispin's day.[1]

I stood there staring at the long row of bayoneted rifles stuck in the sand, a pair of boots in front of each, and in the case of Rangers, a black beret draped across the top. I thought about the "brothers" I knew best—Dominick Pilla, Casey Joyce, and Lorenzo Ruiz. Casey had a wife I'd met named DeAnna, and I grieved for the fact that she would never hold him again. Her phone call with Casey just last Saturday night (Fort Benning time) would be the last of his voice she ever heard.

On Saturday, October 9, Aidid's organization declared a unilateral ceasefire against United Nations forces. He apparently now realized he had gotten into a fight he couldn't win in the end, and it would be better to back off. The city grew quieter. On that same weekend, lo and behold, Chief Warrant Officer Mike Durant, pilot of the second Black Hawk, showed up alive on TV! There he was, broken right leg and all, with a bloody, swollen face from getting clubbed with a rifle butt. But he was alert and coherent.

The interviewer began by calling him a Ranger.

"No, I'm not a Ranger," Mike corrected. "I'm a helicopter pilot. That's a different unit."

"You kill innocent people," the interviewer said.

"Innocent people being killed is not good," Mike diplomatically answered. He was responding the way he'd been trained, which was to bend to your captors' point of view when possible without giving away too much information.

Further questions came driving at him, and he finessed them masterfully. The whole interview took about thirty minutes.

This changed everything. We had an injured man to rescue in the city! Suddenly my fatigue was gone. "Let's go!" we shouted to each other. We were instantly fired up to roll out the gate and blaze a trail to our comrade. When our officers said to hold on just a minute because Oakley might get him released without us having to fight for him, we were almost disappointed.

As it turned out, Aidid did hand over the American pilot to the Red Cross on the following Wednesday, October 14. By then the remaining five bodies were in our possession. The next morning when Mike Durant was helicoptered to our base, we all lined up to form a corridor straight to the transport plane that would take him to Germany. There he came at last, on a stretcher with an IV in his arm, tightly clenching the red beret of his unit in his hand. He waved to us as we wildly cheered and clapped. This man, too, was not left behind.

As the stretcher moved up the ramp into the plane, a song rose up spontaneously along the corridor of men, just a few voices at first, but soon the whole group of us, more than a thousand strong:

> God bless America, land that I love;
> Stand beside her, and guide her,
> Through the night with a light from above . . .[2]

I'm personally a terrible singer, but on that occasion nobody cared. I belted out the words as loudly as anybody. I was proud of my country, proud of Mike's endurance under extreme pressure, proud of our unit, and eager to ask God's blessing on us all as we fought to restore freedom and human decency to this tragic place.

SHOCKING SURPRISE

We were summoned again to a mass formation just a few days later. We lined up in the hot sun wondering what the brass had to say this time. What was the latest word from the Pentagon? Would this be the announcement of our next mission? The new guys who had arrived following the firefight hadn't seen any action yet and were antsy.

Out came Major General Garrison once again, wearing his trademark sunglasses and, of course, the ever-present cigar in his mouth. He wasn't in uniform—just a standard brown T-shirt and a pair of black running shorts. The tall Texan stood there silent for a moment, as if to clear the stage for his words. Then, reaching up with his right hand to take the cigar, he spoke at last in a flat voice:

"The decision has been made to send Task Force Rangers back to the States. In fact, all U.S. forces will leave Somalia by 31 March."

What?

I could not believe my ears, and neither could anybody else. What in the world was the administration back in Washington thinking? After all the blood we shed to get on top of this murderous warlord and gain the upper hand, why were they pulling us out and letting the bad guys have it? The bravery and courage and suffering and dying of eighteen men was going for naught.

I felt absolutely slapped in the face. So did every other Ranger on that airfield. The instant the meeting was dismissed, we exploded in a volley of anger and frustration. Guys threw equipment across the hangar, cursed, and pounded their fists. This made no sense to us at all.

The TV room, a separate space off to one side of the hangar, was quickly jammed with bodies. CNN was already reinforcing what Major General Garrison had announced, complete with pundits and analysts weighing in with "expert" opinions from the other side of the globe. Spliced in was the now wearisome footage of dead soldiers being dragged through the streets, replayed over and over.

I couldn't get through the crush of bodies, so I stood outside of the doorway, stricken with terrible thoughts: *Did we just let our country down? Did we fail to deliver, and so now we're being punished? Did we not do our job?*

If so I would really be ashamed of myself. If I had fallen short of the Ranger Creed in any way, I would be humiliated. I thought back to the legacy room at Ranger headquarters, where the exploits of our regiment during World War II and Korea and all the rest were dramatically displayed. Ranger history had been a very big thing during training, commanding hours and hours of our attention as we memorized names and places and battle operations of the past. Had I failed to follow in the steps of those brave men from years gone by? Was I unworthy to call myself by their name?

What were Dawn and my family back in Iowa thinking right now? They'd probably already gotten the word on American TV. Were they thinking that Jeff and his team fell short?

I agonized over this, even when officers tried to give us pep talks of "Oh, you guys are great, what you did was heroic, you'll be remembered," blah blah blah. I didn't believe them for a minute. In my mind, my country was embarrassed about the firefight—mainly because of the ugly pictures on CNN—and was disciplining the troops for lack of success.

By the next day, my shame had turned to irritation. "Wait just a minute," I said to more than one guy. "Didn't we complete the mission? We were told to go get two of Aidid's senior men; we actually got three. We snagged dozens of others in the same building. When the fight got nasty, we killed hundreds of their militia. [Later estimates came to five hundred of the enemy killed and perhaps twice as many wounded.]

"Yes, all of that cost us eighteen men. Another seventy-three got hurt. But are any of us whining about it? No. Why can't the politicians in Washington buck up and stay the course?"

Soldiers know the consequences of their job. We know we're going to lose people in combat. We don't hold some Pollyanna view that an operation can be completed without blood. We're prepared for consequences.

When we took on the Somalia mission, I didn't think the consequences would be as severe as they turned out to be. But that happens sometimes. It's all part of being an effective defense force the nation can depend upon.

As we Rangers were packing up over the next several days, we heard on TV the beginnings of a public debate back in America on whether the United States had changed its policy unwisely. Were we now going to cut and run every time the going got hard? What did our extraction from Somalia say to every other dictator and thug in the world? That if they could just punch Uncle Sam in the nose hard enough, he'd pack up and go home? It seemed to us that this was just asking for more trouble and mayhem. Now bullies and oppressors all over the globe would be emboldened.

We were a sullen, frustrated unit as we got on the planes to return to the United States near the end of October. Of course we looked forward to seeing our loved ones again—but not under these conditions. We had wanted to return with honor. Instead, we felt dishonored and trivialized. We wondered what our commanders back at Fort Benning, our family members, and the average person on the street would say to us.

DÉJÀ VU

On a personal level, it was a thrill to see Dawn waiting for me as I arrived. "Welcome home, honey!" she cried as I ran toward her, noticing that her tummy was starting to swell now in the fourth month of pregnancy. We hugged and kissed each other and were glad to be together again.

She was very gracious and patient with me through the early weeks, giving me time to readjust to home life. She, along with most military wives, knew that guys sometimes have mental health problems when they return from combat. Fortunately I experienced no nightmares or stress attacks, and I think she deserves a lot of the credit for that. She was such a loving partner.

In the media, however, the analysts were busy pointing out that "not since Vietnam has there been a firefight of this magnitude." The scenes of the bodies of Gary Gordon and Randy Shughart and the others being dragged through the streets were rerun ad nauseam. I got sick of all the pontifications by "experts" who hadn't been there. For the first time in my life, I found myself not wanting people to notice the Ranger tab on my shoulder.

A small group of us was asked to march in the Veterans Day

parade on November 11 that year in New York City. We would carry the colors of the Ranger Regiment right after the national flag at the head of the procession. The five of us flew up the day before to be ready.

The next morning we left the hotel in our dress uniforms and entered a nearby subway station, where we would catch the train to the parade's staging area. Our colors were furled under our arms until the time to bring them out. Suddenly a young man with long hair came up and spit on us! "You bunch of baby killers, what are you doing here?" he shouted, launching into his tirade.

We were shocked. The first of our group to react was a young Ranger who had been Lieutenant Danny McKnight's gunner in Somalia. He flew into a rage. "You don't know what you're talking about, you scum! We were over there defending your freedom, and you obviously don't appreciate it!" He lunged at the protestor and was about to body-slam him onto the subway platform until some of the rest of us restrained him.

Just then the train came, and we all got on. We sat there thinking, *This is what the guys coming back from Vietnam had to endure. It's 1973 all over again, isn't it?* We avoided looking each other in the eyes for the whole ride. Each of us was consumed with our private thoughts.

Later on I did say to the young soldier, "Man, that guy doesn't know. He wasn't where you and I have been. He doesn't know the least bit about what we went through, and he'll never understand it. Even other guys in the service don't fully get it. There's no use trying to tell them, either. You just had to be there."

A few days later, we read in the papers that the Organization of African Unity (the "UN of Africa," so to speak) was holding a peace conference in Nairobi, Kenya, and wanted Mohamed Farrah Aidid to attend on behalf of Somalia. I just about did some spitting of my own when I got to the part in the article that said he would be picked up and flown there on a U.S. Marine helicopter! *We gave our blood and guts to capture that murderer,* I fumed. *And now he gets treated like a player on the international stage? Thanks a lot.* Our nation's public policy had swiveled so quickly that Aidid now had instant legitimacy and status among world leaders.

Before long we learned that all five or six dozen of the captives we had gathered were being gradually released back onto the streets of Mogadishu. They hadn't done anything so bad after all, it seemed. They were welcome to resume their previous roles in the ongoing chaos of the country.

On December 15 that year, Secretary of Defense Les Aspin resigned under fire after less than eleven months in office. He had already admitted his mistake in turning down an early request for tanks and armored vehicles in Somalia. President Clinton, in making the announcement, cited "personal reasons" for Aspin's departure, including his health. The news media had more critical explanations to offer, and we in the Ranger Regiment could hardly disagree.

Several of our own leaders, although not resigning, came to realize that their careers were now stalemated. Promotions just weren't going to happen for the men who had been in charge at Mogadishu. Among those of us who served under them, a bunker mentality began to take root. We didn't try to defend ourselves. We resigned ourselves to a life of being misunderstood. If people wanted to think Task Force Ranger had failed, they could think it. We wouldn't try to argue them out of their belief. We would just go on doing our duty regardless.

Quietly on the side, we tried to pump each other up. We phoned each other or, as the Internet came alive during the mid-1990s, sent each other e-mails to say, "Hey, man, I know what you did over there, and I appreciate it. I'm proud to know you." Nobody else was going to say it, but we would.

It wasn't fun. Anybody who lives with a cloud over their head knows what I'm talking about. You can tackle just about any challenge in life if you know the meaning attached to it. If you're convinced that the task is relevant and important, you will pour out your soul to make it happen. You'll go to the extreme.

But if somebody changes the rules in the middle of the effort—if the meaning goes away—your motivation is ruined. You feel like a sucker. You were straining every muscle and burning midnight oil for something that apparently didn't matter after all. You don't know how to process this.

Nothing quite drains a life like meaninglessness. I thought to myself about the contrast between serving my government and serving my Lord. My role as a soldier was subject to this kind of undercutting. But what Christ had asked me to do for him would matter forever, even after death. It was permanently significant. I would never have to worry that he would someday say, "Oh, just forget it."

THE RAMIFICATIONS

On April 6, 1994—less than seven months after we had returned from Somalia—an airplane carrying the presidents of two other troubled African nations, Rwanda and Burundi, was shot down as it prepared to land. Both presidents were killed. This was the trigger that unleashed a bloodbath in Rwanda between the Hutu and Tutsi tribes, who had been quarrelling with each other for a long time.

The majority Hutus immediately assumed that the Tutsi rebels had assassinated their leader and responded with fierce assaults.

Would outside nations step in to separate the warring parties? Would the United States or any other world power intervene in this deadly situation?

Not after Mogadishu.

The United Nations and its member states basically sat on their hands and did nothing as a genocide exploded. In just one hundred days, some eight hundred thousand people were slaughtered. The rivers ran red with the blood of men, women, and children. (The 2004 movie *Hotel Rwanda* tells the story through the eyes of one courageous Hutu businessman, married to a Tutsi wife, who tried to save lives by hiding people in his facility. The film received three Academy Award nominations.)

Two years later, on August 1, 1996, Mohamed Farrah Aidid died of gunshot wounds he had received the week before in a battle with another Somali clan. The man whom some world leaders thought should be appeased and ushered toward leadership of his people was felled by the violence he had encouraged throughout his career.

Twenty-four hours later, on August 2, 1996, Major General William Garrison announced his immediate retirement from the army. I for one was sorry to see him go. He had been a father figure for Task Force Ranger—approachable, unpretentious, levelheaded, almost soft-spoken. He didn't demand the usual ruffles and flourishes when he walked into the room. I respected him more than any senior leader I knew.

I wish he could have stayed on for three more years, until Mark Bowden's book *Black Hawk Down* came out in 1999. Subtitled *A Story of Modern War*, this remarkable chronicle by a *Philadelphia*

Inquirer reporter finally turned the tide of public opinion. The perception of our efforts changed almost overnight. The true story of what we were up against, the constraints we endured, and the accomplishments we produced was finally told. I especially appreciated such lines as, "The truth is, Task Force Ranger came within minutes of pulling off its mission on October 3 without a hitch. If Black Hawk *Super Six One* [Wolcott's] had not been hit, the 'bad' choices by Garrison would have been called bold."[3]

The book hit the *New York Times* best-seller list and spawned a whole new appreciation. People came up to me and said, "I had no idea. Now I get it. You guys were awesome over there."

My mother called me, bawling. I hadn't mentioned to her that my name was in the book in several places, knowing her antiwar sentiments from long ago. Somebody else told her that her son was in the account and she should read it. Now she was aghast. "You never told me you went through all this! You never told me how hard it was!"

"Well, Mom," I replied, "I'm not sure how a son tells his mother this kind of stuff. It's not something you enjoy talking about. I guess I just thought you'd be better off not knowing about it."

"Are you going to be okay?" she asked in a worried tone. "Can I do anything to help you?"

"No, I'm all right, Mom," I answered. "Seriously, I'm fine."

Two years later, in 2001, the movie appeared, featuring Sam Shepard (in the role of Major General Garrison) plus Josh Hartnett, Ewan McGregor, Tom Sizemore, and other first-rate actors. It won Academy Awards for Best Film Editing and Best Sound. Now even more people, both inside and outside of the military, changed their minds about the Ranger Regiment and what we did. We could hold our heads high once again.

In the final analysis, what others thought of me wasn't the ultimate test. I convinced myself that I did my duty in Somalia as a Ranger. I kept the Ranger Creed, especially the "E" stanza:

Energetically will I meet the enemies of my country. I shall defeat them on the field of battle, for I am better trained and will fight with all my might. *Surrender* is not a Ranger word. I will never leave a fallen comrade to fall into the hands of the enemy, and under no circumstances will I ever embarrass my country.

I had served my nation's cause with determination, and I had nothing to feel guilty about. I refused to yield to the pop opinions about our mission. Time had validated our efforts after all.

A chapel service in the deserts of Fort Irwin, California.

Dawn and children welcome daddy home to Fort Bragg, North Carolina, after a very long separation.

Eleven

THE BEST?

AFTER SOMALIA I DID NOT HAVE TO DEPLOY OVERSEAS again for the next ten years. I got to be home for the birth of Aaron on April 27, 1994, which was the fulfillment of a dream for Dawn and me. His brother Jacob came along in early 1996, and a year and a half later we welcomed Joseph as well. Our house was filling up fast.

We had always talked about having a lively family of kids, and after the initial delay of more than two years following our wedding, we were now receiving the answer to our prayers. It helped that we were not having to move as often as most army families. Fort Benning was pretty much the "Ranger capital," and that's where we got to stay, with the same doctors, hospital, and other valuable services.

My daily work following Mogadishu was as an RIP (Ranger Indoctrination Program) instructor. I took one batch after another of volunteers for the regiment and put them through eighteen days of torture to see if they were cut out to be the best.

At the same time, I began training for a challenge that happens every year on the last weekend of April—the David E. Grange Jr.

Best Ranger Competition. It's the army's version of an Olympic decathlon, only about five times harder. Or to give you another comparison: the world-famous Ironman competition in Hawaii every year has three parts—a 2.4-mile swim in the ocean, a 112-mile bike ride, and a full marathon run of 26.2 miles. The winner in recent years finished all this in just a little more than eight hours. The Best Ranger Competition, in contrast, involves some twenty-two major physical events, a dozen or more technical challenges, and an array of shooting. The whole ordeal runs basically nonstop over *three days* and *two nights*. You start at 5:00 a.m. on a Friday and get to the finish line around 5:00 p.m. Sunday, having eaten nothing more than an occasional MRE. No outside food is allowed; spectators are kept behind ropes so they can't pass any food or drink. Any competitor caught cheating is immediately thrown out.

Call me a masochist, but I wanted to try it! This would be a fresh opportunity to put myself to the test, to see how good I really was, or wasn't. I looked down the list of individual events and knew I wasn't the fastest guy in the world by any means, but maybe my overall endurance would carry me through.

Another unique angle of Best Ranger is that you compete in two-man teams. You and a partner work side-by-side, and your combined score is what counts. Thus, two men are named Best Ranger of the year. I chose to compete with a great friend who was with me in Somalia, Sergeant Aaron Weaver. He was a short guy from the Florida beaches whose boyish looks and bronze tan could fool you. In fact he was not only strong but also lightning fast; he'd been a sprinter in high school.

Following is what we were in for.

DAY ONE (FRIDAY)

Right off the bat, a set of PT tests:

- All the sit-ups you can do in two minutes
- All the push-ups you can do in two minutes
- Pull-ups to the point of exhaustion

Immediately you're shuttled to a rifle range with *moving* targets. You get fifty bullets, and you have to hit at least thirty-five targets (while your muscles are still quivering from the pull-ups). If you don't make thirty-five, you're immediately dropped from the competition.

Next comes a parachute jump for accuracy. You load into a helicopter right there on the rifle range, pull on your equipment, and fly off to a drop zone where two distinct circles are marked on the ground. They're some fifteen feet in diameter, but from a thousand feet in the air they look like pinholes. You and your teammate must each land in one of the circles. If you miss, you must scramble like crazy to get into the circle as fast as you can, because you're being clocked.

Then it's back to shooting again on a series of ranges, only this time you're switching quickly from one weapon to another: an M-60 machine gun, then a grenade launcher, a SAW (squad automatic weapon), a rifle, and a pistol.

Next up: a ten-kilometer canoe race. Again, you can get kicked out of everything on this event if you don't complete the course within a certain time.

From the time the last team finishes their canoeing, you get approximately a two-hour break before starting the all-night road march, which is the real elimination event. Saddled with a heavy pack, you march along an unknown route for an unknown distance. It could be twenty miles, it could be thirty—you're not told what to expect. In fact the contest managers themselves don't know how long they'll keep you going; they just wait to see how many teams drop out from exhaustion or get so far behind that they'll never finish in a reasonable amount of time. When half the teams have failed in either of these ways, the road march is declared to be over. Until then you just keep going and going.

This makes it hard to strategize. During the early miles, you want to get out there and really move—but you don't know how carefully to pace yourself, because you don't know the overall length. You could fly through the first ten or twelve miles and push yourself over the edge, so that you have nothing left for the rest—however long that turns out to be.

This march takes four to six hours, lapping over into . . .

DAY TWO (SATURDAY)

After a thirty-minute break, while it's still dark in the early hours of the morning, a series of technical events begin.

You and your teammate are brought to a poncho that's covering a pile of disassembled weapons parts on the ground. The pieces of four or five different guns are all jumbled together in a heap underneath. When the poncho comes off, you have five minutes to put all the weapons back together correctly. Some of them, such as an M-60 machine gun, are quite complex and would under normal conditions take more than two minutes to assemble on their own.

Then you're given a radio that you must put into operation, encode a message, and transmit it to someone on the other end, again within a time limit.

Next comes a demolitions event. You plan how to blow up a target—say, a tree or a piece of steel—taking measurements, then preparing the charge correctly and putting it in place.

As soon as daybreak comes, you're back to shooting again, this time with a pistol.

There's also a "call for fire" test, in which you must give accurate instructions for return artillery from your support force some distance away.

The "move under direct fire" event requires you to advance against a sniper (firing lasers, not live ammo) and take him out before he gets you.

Sometime on Day Two you're sure to get a couple of "mystery events"—oddball things that nobody's heard of in advance. One year it was throwing a hatchet at a log a hundred feet away, like back in the pioneer days. Another year it was a performance of hand and arm signals used in warfare when it's too loud to hear. You can't prepare for this kind of challenge; you just have to give it your best shot at the moment.

Soon comes the Prussik Climb—ascending a fixed rope sixty feet into the air, traversing across a horizontal frame and then rappelling back down another rope on the opposite end. (Prussik is the type of knot used on the big rope.) Sixty seconds is normal for this event; the winners do it in about thirty-five or even less.

Around eight o'clock that evening begins the all-night land navigation test. You're given a map with a goal to reach thirty or forty miles away, and you've got to get there by eight o'clock the next morning. To be honest, it's nearly impossible. Most teams get only partway. If you fail to make minimum progress, you can again be dropped from the competition right there.

This is the second night in a row with no sleep.

Day Three (Sunday)

The third day begins with a two-mile obstacle course—ladders to climb, ropes to jump over, barbed wire to crawl under. Each team is timed.

Next comes a water confidence test, in which you move out onto a log, then swing on a rope out over water, drop forty feet, swim to shore, then run up a hundred-foot ladder, and slide down a fixed cable—again while somebody is timing you.

Now that you're already soaking wet, you get to do a "helo-cast." You load onto a helicopter that flies you out over water. There, with all of your equipment tightly wrapped, you jump out. Once in the water, you pull your gear behind you as you swim to a finish line on the beach, where you place a demolitions charge.

Last of all comes a 2.7-mile run in full uniform and boots, carrying all your equipment.

In between these events, you may or may not have the chance to sprawl on the ground and catch a few minutes of sleep. It depends on whether you finished the previous event quickly or slowly. Soon enough in any case, somebody will be coming over to kick you in the ribs and say, "Hey, it's your turn for the next event!"

The scoring system is complex, with more points allotted for the harder events. You really can't afford to back off on any of them. You have to push hard all three days in order to have a hope of winning.

AWARD CEREMONY (MONDAY MORNING)

You go home and collapse Sunday night, then return at 9:00 a.m. Monday for the announcement of the winning team. You don't get a personal trophy, you don't get a badge to add to your dress uniform, and you don't win any money. All you get is the prestige of being known as a Best Ranger for the rest of your military career. Your name goes on a plaque that resides in the National Infantry Center at Fort Benning. Your commanding officer has reason to smile (and brag) about producing the army's best soldiers.

SO CLOSE

Ranger and other airborne-unit commanders, in fact, feel a certain amount of pressure to see their men do well in this competition, to the point that they provide time off to train for it. If selected to compete, Rangers basically got three months—February, March, and April—away from our regular duties to get ready. Day after day, Aaron and I were running, swimming, biking, and road-marching. Sometimes we worked together, other times separately. But we incessantly checked up on each other. "Hey, man, how far did you run today?" "Are you biking this week?" "How long did you road-march yesterday?"

We knew that other unit commanders were giving their guys even more than three months to train. This competition was open to the entire military, and if you could capture the title of Best Ranger even if you weren't in the Ranger Regiment, you really had bragging rights. We Rangers definitely did not like to have to listen to that.

I knew Aaron and I weren't likely to win that first year (1994), because the competition is just too complex. Contestants need to go through it a time or two before they can figure out what is coming. The competition included ten different Ranger teams plus another forty or so from other parts of the military.

To our amazement, however, we started hearing sometime during Day Two that we were in second place, and not by all that much margin. This was unheard of for a rookie team.

We hit a couple of snags on the third day and wound up in fourth place. At the awards ceremony on Monday morning, Aaron and I looked each other in the eye and came to the same decision simultaneously: "We're doing this thing again next year!"

In 1995 expectations ran high for us among the regiment. The strongest Ranger competitor from the year before had left the unit and so would not be in it this time. Everybody began looking our way.

We felt the pressure that winning was the only way to prove the point of our three training months to our fellow soldiers. If we didn't win, they could always say we'd just been messing around those months, hanging out and getting a tan and building muscles instead of doing our normal jobs. That would not have been true, but it was an easy conclusion for the guys to draw.

At the end of Day One in 1995, Aaron and I were in third place among the fifty or so teams. People were starting to talk about us on the sidelines: "Hey, those two were close last year, remember? Struecker and Weaver have a real chance." The longer we kept going on Day Two and into Day Three, the more we seemed to gain, as other teams burned themselves out or made mistakes.

But on the helo-cast jump, one of the ropes on our equipment pack got caught on a piece of steel inside the aircraft just as I shoved the pack out toward the water. The pack jerked hard, slicing the rope in two. Aaron and I jumped into the water, but now had no efficient way to tow this pack toward the finish line. We ended up having to swim with one hand while pulling it along behind us with the other.

I thought about biting the short stub of rope with my teeth in order to have two hands for swimming. But it wasn't even long enough for that. We ended up losing a fair amount of time on the helo-cast. We dropped back to fourth place, which is where we finished.

Aaron and I were proud of having just *finished* the competition, which was more than about 80 percent of the other teams could say. But we were disappointed not to improve on our rating from the year before, even though a lot of people patted us on the back for making a good effort.

A PERSONAL FAVOR

During the coming year, Aaron decided to leave the army. When the 1996 Best Ranger Competition came around, I wasn't interested. I'd already put myself to this test twice. Besides, I was extremely busy with our growing family plus some night classes I was taking. When guys asked me, "Hey, Struecker, are you going for Best Ranger again?" I'd answer, "No, not this time." I didn't add on all the reasons.

January rolled around and teams began showing up from the other Ranger bases at Fort Lewis, Washington, and Savannah, Georgia. They plunged into rigorous training, just as I'd done the two years before. The rest of us watched them, and it didn't seem like we had a clear front-runner in the batch.

Weeks went by. One day in early March, Colonel William J. Leszczynski Jr., commander of the entire Ranger Regiment, called me into his office for a talk.

"Sergeant Struecker, I was just wondering why you're not entering the Best Ranger Competition this year."

I debated how much to say. "Sir," I finally answered, "I've got a lot going on at work right now, and I'm very busy with my family. I just don't feel like I should be carving out the time to train—plus I'm already more than six weeks behind the other guys who started back in January. It's too late to jump in now, isn't it?"

"Sergeant, you know the Ranger Regiment hasn't had a winner the last two years. It was an Eighty-second Airborne team in '94 and then Twenty-fifth Infantry Division last year. We need to get this title back in Ranger hands." He paused a moment, then delivered the punch line: "If you would consider competing on behalf of the Ranger Regiment, I would see it as a personal favor."

What was I going to say to my commanding officer?

"Well . . . ," I said, fumbling for words, "to be honest with you, sir, I'm not sure I can give you an immediate answer. I need to go home and talk to my wife, if that's acceptable."

I could tell he was surprised at my hesitation. "Okay—just let me know," he replied, standing up. "I'll hear from you tomorrow, right?"

"Yes, sir."

That evening at home I said, "Dawn, you'll never guess what happened today. The regimental commander called me into his office and directly asked me to do Best Ranger again. He said that without me they basically don't have a strong team. I was, like, speechless!"

She looked down at baby Jacob in her arms, only a month old. Quietly she said, "I thought you weren't going to do it again."

"Yeah, that's right—I did say that," I answered. "It's just hard to look your commanding officer in the eye and tell him no."

"I understand," she replied. "What do you want to do?"

"I guess I'm torn. It definitely wouldn't be the same without Aaron Weaver this time. And I'm already way behind on training. I've got plenty to do here at home and everything else. But on the other hand, I'd kind of like to take on the challenge again . . ."

We prayed together that night for direction. We honestly didn't know which way to go.

The next morning after breakfast, Dawn summarized her feelings: "If you want to do it, Jeff, I'm okay with that. I understand the pressure you're facing. It means the boys and I won't see much of you for the next six or seven weeks. But after that, it will be over. You make the call."

I gave her a hug, and once again I was reminded what a tremendously dedicated and spiritually mature wife the Lord had given me.

That day I went to see Colonel Leszczynski again. "Okay, sir, I will enter the competition as asked—on one condition," I announced. "I want the teams formed on a regiment-wide basis, instead of battalion by battalion. We'll get together, *all* of us Rangers, and hold a pre-competition to determine who's strongest. Then let the teams match up regardless of unit." (In the past, the First Battalion formed its own teams, the Second, the Third, and the regimental headquarters on a separate basis. This sometimes resulted in a strong man being paired with a noticeably weaker teammate because that's all the unit had to offer.)

"You've got a deal," the commander replied.

"Sir, it won't be as easy as it sounds," I offered. "You're going to get flak from the battalion commanders or the command sergeants major, calling you up to complain, 'So why is my guy training with somebody from a different battalion?'"

"Don't worry about it," he answered. "I'll take care of it."

Soon the new plan was put into action. We held our minicompetition about three weeks later. I surprised myself by coming in first. In second place was a mountain of a man from the Second Battalion out at Fort Lewis, who had done well the year before. Specialist Isaac Gmazel was much bigger and more muscular than I was; I could tell that with a big rucksack on his back, he'd be phenomenal. We would be Ranger Team One. The rest of the Ranger teams fell into place according to the standings from the tryout—ten teams in all.

We soon found out the 1996 competition was going to throw us a curve ball. The various events were going to be scrambled from their traditional order—and there would be no advance listing. We wouldn't know if we were going to shoot first or road-march or do a parachute jump. We wouldn't be told what was coming next even during the three days of the competition. We just had to show up and be ready for anything.

The organizers also announced that for the first time there would be no posting of records during the event. We wouldn't know where we ranked in the standings until the very end. We would just have to keep driving.

Isaac and I looked at each other and said, "Okay, this is crazy! But let's give it our best shot and see what happens."

In the Dark

It was still dark that early Friday morning when we all lined up to begin. We were promptly loaded onto helicopters for a trip to north Georgia. There a ropes course was first up. Next came something called "traverse and rescue"—I'd never even heard of it! What was this event all about? I was greatly relieved to hear Isaac say, "Oh, yeah,

I used to do this before I joined the army. Here's how it works . . ." We had five minutes for him to give me a crash briefing, and then we jumped into scaling a steep cliff using a set of fixed ropes.

By midmorning we had been thrown into the twelve-hour land navigation challenge. It was nice to be doing this in daylight instead of overnight like the year before—except that the weather was unusually hot for late April. Fully half of the fifty-some teams flunked out by that evening.

As for the survivors, we got a forty-five minute rest to get some water and change our socks, then immediately struck out on the long road march with full packs—unannounced route, undetermined length. Isaac's brute strength really shone here, and I did my best to keep up with him. We were in the dark at least three different ways: it was nighttime, we didn't know how long we'd have to march, and we didn't know where we stood in the competition. We just kept chugging.

Sometime in the wee hours of the morning we were told we could stop. Only about ten teams were still in the competition. Back on the helicopters we traveled to Fort Benning. Obviously none of us had trouble sleeping on this short flight.

Day Two brought shooting, technical events, the Prussik Climb, and that night, *another* twelve hours of land navigation. I'd never heard of an event being repeated in the Best Ranger Competition. I wasn't complaining, however, because this happened to be one of my better events. I enjoyed the challenge of getting from here to there across unfamiliar terrain.

By Day Three, we kind of knew what hadn't been covered yet, so we were half-expecting the obstacle course, the water confidence test, and the helo-cast. Along the way I received some bootleg information from a friend on the competition staff. "Hey, Jeff," he whispered, "do you realize you and Isaac are in first place right now?"

"No way!"

"It's true. In fact you guys are so far ahead on points that the only way you could lose is if you die or one of you gets hurt. Even if you finish last on every remaining event, your lead will still hold up!"

"You're kidding me."

I pulled Isaac off to the side and told him what I'd just heard. "What do you want to do?" I asked. "Shall we back off just a notch and save our strength?"

"No," my partner replied. "Let's keep giving everything we've got right to the end." By now we were out of food and even water. We were scooping up swamp water to stay hydrated. Still we agreed to keep pushing ourselves to the very end.

The full PT test—normally the opening event—turned out to be the finale this year. While doing push-ups, I glanced sideways at Isaac. He was just steaming away—up, down, up, down, up, down. We both soon moved on to pull-ups, which was a go-to-exhaustion event. We were pulling, pulling, pulling—and I started to realize that nobody was still going but us. We'd outperformed every other team in this event.

Maybe we're really going to win this thing! I thought. *Maybe my friend wasn't just blowing smoke about us being in first place.*

Isaac and I finally dropped down to the ground and headed toward the finish line with the rest. A crowd awaited us. We could smell the barbecue in the air. We could see the broadcast booth of the local radio station doing live coverage.

I turned in relief toward Dawn, who was holding Jacob, while two-year-old Aaron jumped up and down in front of her. "Good job, Daddy!" he cried in his tiny voice. Dawn had a big smile on her face as she said, "I'm proud of you, honey!" We all grabbed each other for a hug. Then she handed me a Gatorade liter, which I downed in one gulp.

Suddenly the fatigue came rolling over me. I bent down, my hands on my knees, and started crying. I could not believe that Isaac and I had maybe actually won this thing. When I got control of myself, I slapped Isaac on the back and said, "Hey! Let's get some food!" With that, we headed straight for the buffet.

The announcer's voice came over the loudspeakers: "The points are now tallied, and we have the results. The winners of the Best Ranger award for 1996 are—Jeff Struecker and Isaac Gmazel!"

The next morning at nine o'clock, we were back for the formal awards ceremony. General Gordon Sullivan, army chief of staff from Washington, was there to speak. The commanders of all the units that sent teams filed in. With a great deal of pomp, Isaac and I were called forward to receive General Sullivan's congratulations. He handed each of us an engraved Gold Cup pistol from the Colt Corporation worth several thousand dollars.

Ranger teams won first, third, fourth, seventh, eighth, and ninth places that year. Colonel Leszczynski was a happy man. He was the first to shake my hand, almost pushing Dawn out of the way to get there.

A couple of hours later back at home, I was winding down when Dawn asked in a slightly mischievous way, "So, do you think this is finally out of your system now? Are you done with Best Ranger?"

"Yes, Dawn, it's finally over!" I quickly replied. "Never again."

At least I would never *compete* again. I had no choice but to talk about it in media interviews for the next year. Everybody from ESPN to Associated Press to UPI to *Outdoor Life* magazine wanted to do features. Isaac and I were invited to go on the *Late Show with David Letterman*. Even *The New Yorker* ran a big story on the Best Ranger Competition—not exactly their usual fare.

All this attention forced me to give up my personal "no-media" policy, which I had held for nine years, ever since joining the army. After all, Rangers don't blab about what they do. We conduct unusual operations, and we don't want a lot of attention. We especially don't appreciate media that distort our efforts.

I had asked Dawn not to talk to reporters over the years. When anyone put a microphone in front of my face after Kuwait or Somalia, I always said, "I have no comment for you," and just walked away.

Now as Best Ranger for 1996, that clearly wasn't going to work. The army wanted me to speak publicly.

I changed my policy at that juncture. I said to myself that I'd be open and available for interviews—including the part about Jesus Christ being my ultimate source of strength. I figured if media people wanted to talk to me, I would give them the full picture of what makes me tick and what had kept me going through every hard test as a soldier. I wouldn't sound like a religious freak, but neither would I hide the importance of my faith in God.

I prayed a lot about how to do this with credibility. I asked my church to pray for me, too. I sincerely wanted to give God the credit every time, rather than just exalting Jeff Struecker.

I also wanted to share the honor with the Ranger Regiment, which had been so essential to my success. I asked for a meeting with Colonel Leszczynski so I could donate my Gold Cup pistol to the regiment. He wouldn't accept it at first and tried to tell me I'd regret giving it up later. The next day I went back and finally convinced him I was serious.

In order to go on display at regimental headquarters, the pistol had to be de-milled, so that it could never be fired. It is still there to this day.

When people ask, "Hey, where's that pistol you won?" I say, "Well, there's a story about that. I gave it away—to the Ranger Regiment. I could never have won Best Ranger without the training and support of the entire unit. And I could never have won without the strength and courage I drew from my faith in Jesus Christ. He's the real Hero, as far as I'm concerned."

In fact that spiritual connection would become even more visible to the public in the months and years to come.

Captain Jeff Struecker and Specialist Isaac Gmazel holding up the winning pistols after the 1996 Best Ranger Competition.

Twelve

A Hard Right Turn

The fame of Best Ranger was invigorating, of course. But in my quiet moments when the interviewers left and I found time to reflect, my mind would return to the hours right after Black Hawk Down. One guy after another had stopped by my cot to ask serious questions about eternity. I had tried to answer them as best I could, and I began wondering if I'd do more of this in future years.

I kept thinking about that on the long flight home from Somalia—when I wasn't fuming inside about getting jerked out of Somalia prematurely. Through that winter and spring I pondered the subject more than once. I didn't raise it with Dawn, however, because I didn't really know my own mind. Everything was pretty hazy for me.

I just felt I'd seen and done nearly everything I wanted to do as a Ranger NCO in combat. And this last mission had not achieved the objective of overthrowing the warlord anyway. Could God be leading me to do something different with my life?

I wanted to make more of an impact for God's kingdom. I wanted to have a greater influence on others, whether my fellow

Rangers or the kid bagging groceries at the store. My nightly Bible reading became increasingly alive to me, and I started a weekly Bible study in my unit. But when I tried to share my excitement about God's Word, it seemed that others were ho-hum about it. They didn't see what I saw. Maybe I needed some help with how to communicate.

Sometime around June 1994, I stopped by to see Phil Wright, the Ranger chaplain. "Can I talk to you about something?" I asked, poking my head into his office.

"Sure, come on in. Sit down," he said warmly.

"Sir, I just need your advice on something."

"Okay. What's going on?" In the back of his mind, he was no doubt thinking, *This guy's probably still having problems from Somalia.*

"Well," I answered, stopping for a breath and then continuing, "I think God is calling me to the ministry."

Chaplain Wright almost fell out of his chair. I could see in his eyes that I had caught him totally off guard. He didn't utter a word for a long time. Finally he softly asked, "Are you serious?"

After all the whole Ranger personality—tough, aggressive, physical, and usually raw around the edges—didn't have much in common with clergy life.

"Yes, I'm serious," I answered. "I've been thinking about this for months, ever since Mogadishu. It was amazing how many guys came around asking questions about God that next day." I went on to give some of the details and a couple of examples.

He listened to me and took another deep breath. Finally he asked, "How much college do you have?"

"None, sir," I answered. "I entered the army straight out of high school."

"Okay, then," Chaplain Wright replied. "Your first step would be to go back to school and get a bachelor's degree. You can't even start seminary without that. We've got a couple of college options right here in the Columbus area, you know. You could do night classes starting in the fall."

I nodded. I could tell he believed me after all. He talked some more about following God's call in my life and then closed by offering to pray with me.

By this time Dawn and I had immersed ourselves in the life of Fairview Baptist Church. We'd become members and both joined the choir, which in my case was more of a liability than an asset for the church. We were in church every time the doors were open, not only on Sundays but Wednesdays as well. We were hungry for the things of God, reading books, and seeking to grow in our spiritual lives. Henry Blackaby's *Experiencing God* became a best seller around that time, and it pierced my heart like an arrow. Its subtitle was *Knowing and Doing the Will of God.*

We greatly admired Pastor Tommy Green, the most lovable man I'd ever met. I talked Dawn into inviting Tommy and his wife, Anita, over to our apartment for dinner, even though we didn't have much furniture. We would need to sit around the coffee table in the living room as we ate. But we were a typical army couple, and we knew they'd understand.

The night before the dinner, I had to come clean with Dawn about what was on my mind for discussion.

"Honey, um, what I'm really thinking about is, when the Greens come over tomorrow night, I just want to ask them about something. I think God is calling me into the ministry."

She froze. It was like the moment back in Iowa when I had shocked her with my marriage proposal, only worse. Of all the surprises I had pulled on her in our life together, this had to be the most stunning.

"You *what?* What are you talking about?"

"I know it sounds crazy. But I can't get away from it. Ever since Somalia, I've been thinking about what really counts for eternity. The only thing that really matters in this world is people's destiny. If they don't have a relationship with Jesus, they're in big trouble. I think I want to try to help them discover him."

She gasped. "Jeff—have you forgotten that your name just came up for promotion to sergeant first class? And we're moving in a few months to get a real house on Fort Benning, instead of this little apartment? How on earth—? I don't get it."

"I know it's pretty wild," I admitted. "I would have to get a lot more education."

She shook her head in amazement. "Does that mean I'd have to become a pastor's wife?" This was perhaps the biggest jolt of all, given her Catholic background, which included no such role at all; priests didn't marry. The alarm on her face told me I was blowing all the circuitry in her brain.

"I don't know what to say about that," I replied. "A lot of things don't have answers right now. I just know God's talking to me about a change. What's that verse in Jeremiah where he said he just had to speak because the word of the Lord was like fire in his bones? That's how I feel. I can't get away from it."

It's amazing she didn't refuse to cook dinner the next night, knowing what I planned to say. But she was gracious enough to put on a nice meal. After the main course was finished and we were having coffee, I began. "Tommy, I need to talk to you about something."

"Uh-oh, this is never good," he said with a grin that let us know he was kidding.

"I think God is calling me to the ministry."

He and Anita sat there speechless at first, just as Chaplain Wright had done. Dawn stared at the floor.

"Well, tell me about this," the pastor finally said. "What brought all this about?"

I went into my story. Soon he came back with the same question I'd heard before: "How much college do you have?" I admitted I had none. "Okay, that's the first step," he said.

Anita, who happened to be a professor at Columbus Technical College, began giving me advice about how to get started in school. I soaked up the details of application and scheduling. Tommy added what I already knew, that this undergraduate work would have to precede any seminary enrollment.

"By the way," I asked, "where's the best seminary?"

"I would recommend the Southern Baptist Theological Seminary in Louisville, Kentucky," he replied. "It's very strong academically and definitely has a conservative, biblical approach." In the back of my mind I thought that this also would put us closer to our families in the Midwest—if we could ever get there. But such a goal was a long, long way off.

I was pulled back to the present moment by his next question. "When you talk about 'the ministry,' Jeff, what kind of work do you think God is calling you to do? A military chaplain, or something else?"

"I don't know. Could be the pastorate. Could be as a missionary. I can't say for sure."

We prayed together that evening before they left. While cleaning up the dishes afterward, I could tell that Dawn was a little more agreeable to the idea. She still had a ton of questions, but she wasn't going to fight me on this.

UNDER THE RADAR

Neither of us breathed a word to family or friends during the next months. I definitely was not ready to talk about such a crazy idea at work. I knew Rangers would be absolutely shocked. They would view it as a hard right turn in my career that would result in a messy crash.

That fall of 1994, I enrolled for night classes at Columbus State University, which was within a mile of our apartment. When we moved onto Fort Benning, I transferred the next semester to Troy State University, which had an on-post campus just for soldiers and their families. It was normal for enlisted men such as myself to try and advance their education in the evenings. Nobody guessed at *why* I was doing this.

Through all the Best Ranger Competitions and other events of 1995 and 1996, I kept my mouth shut. I made the rank of sergeant first class, which helped put a little more money in our pocket for tuition and books. I kept plugging away at school, gathering credits toward my bachelor's degree. Dawn was very supportive to let me study when I needed to do so, even though she had her hands full with babies. She came around to accept the idea of a career change for me.

After winning Best Ranger in 1996, I was all the more uneasy about telling the regiment where I was headed. The win had given me a larger-than-life reputation. As an RIP instructor, I was a very strict disciplinarian who sent dozens of guys back to their home units each week.

Meanwhile, senior officers in the Ranger Regiment began talking to me about more responsibility. "We need to move you back across the street [from regimental headquarters to the Third Battalion] to become a platoon sergeant," they said. "That will put you in line for the next promotion, to master sergeant."

I was getting boxed in. How in the world was I going to reveal that I had a different future in mind? If my long-ago lifestyle adjustments in language, drinking, and music had shocked the troops, the image of Jeff Struecker becoming a minister would absolutely cause an explosion. It would be like saying I'd decided to become a kindergarten teacher. It would be beyond all comprehension.

I have to admit, I was afraid of the fallout. Would the army think I'd gone soft all of a sudden? That I couldn't take the heat anymore? That the Somalia firefight had messed with my mind and I couldn't face the enemy again? I kept stalling.

Finally in late 1996, I went to see Command Sergeant Major Mike Hall. I sat down in his office, took a deep breath, and said, "I can't do it."

"Can't do what?"

"Can't take this job across the street."

"Why not?"

"Well, you're not going to believe this, but—God is calling me into the ministry."

He stared at me for a minute, then shot back: "What the *** are you talking about? You're one of my best NCOs. You just won Best Ranger! Now you're going off to be a *missionary?*"

"No, that's not what I said. I said I was being called to the ministry. I don't know what kind of ministry that will be."

He slumped back in his chair. "So, like, when are you going to do this?" he wanted to know.

"Well, actually, I've been in school for the past two-and-a-half years, working on my bachelor's. I'll get done with that by next summer. After that I don't know what the next step will be; I'm still figuring that out. But I do know beyond any doubt that God wants me to do this."

I knew he had the power to make my life miserable from this moment on. He sat staring at me for the longest time. I was greatly relieved when he finally opened his mouth to say, "Okay, what do I need to do to help you make this happen?"

"Right now, Sergeant Major, I don't know. I'll keep you posted, okay?" I walked out of his office with a load off my shoulders.

Ranger Gone Weird

The word spread across Fort Benning like wildfire. Everybody had already known that I was an up-front Christian. Some of them even called me a Jesus freak. But this took the matter to a whole new level.

I couldn't walk into the Ranger dining facility or down a barracks hall without hearing conversation behind my back. "Hey, did you hear what Struecker's going to do? He's going to be a *missionary!* Weird, man."

"You mean, like, shave his head and go hand out booklets at the Atlanta airport? Incredible!" Guys would roar with laughter and ridicule.

I tried to correct the worst assumptions, explaining that I honestly didn't know yet what kind of ministry I'd be doing. But it was an uphill battle. The banter went on for months.

One day at breakfast, a good friend of mine said, "Come on, Jeff, shoot straight with me. Was it Somalia? Did that shake you up? Is that what's causing all this?"

Again I tried to set the record straight. During the next six months, I probably did not have more than five people in uniform come up to me and say, "I understand" or "Good for you" or "Hey, God bless you, Jeff." Chaplain Phil Wright did, of course. I can hardly think of any others. The overwhelming comment was: "What are you doing *that* for? I thought you were a soldier."

Toward spring, I started hearing more of "So, are you leaving the army? You've already got close to ten years of service; you're halfway to retirement, man. What's the matter with you?"

It was tough to stand against the tide of military opinion. I didn't want anyone to think I was wimping out. They were drawing all sorts of conclusions about me that weren't real positive. And that made me uneasy inside. I was worried about my reputation—something I now regret.

I needed to realize more fully at that point in my life what Jesus said: "If you refuse to take up your cross and follow me, you are not worthy of being mine" (Matthew 10:38). I had to be willing to accept public misunderstanding and humiliation in order to fulfill my purpose before God. It wasn't easy, even as it wasn't for Jesus. But it was necessary.

On the outside I was affirmed at church for what I was planning to do. My sister Jenny and her husband now lived nearby in Georgia and had become active believers. They congratulated us. So did Diane, Dawn's twin sister, and her husband back in Iowa, who likewise had come to personal faith in Christ.

The rest of the family members on both sides were not so thrilled. Dawn's mother saw this as an even stronger lurch in the Protestant direction. My mother basically didn't get it any more than she had comprehended her son joining the army in the first place. It seemed that Jeff was out on yet another wild tangent. My dad, though nominally Lutheran, didn't see the point either. The same was true of my older sister Angie and my brother, Troy.

Dawn and I tried to take all this in stride, continuing to move in the direction God had called. We still did not know at this point the kind of ministry we would ultimately do. We had to figure out the more immediate challenges of finishing college and then getting ourselves to Louisville.

Reading the Bible in army green and camouflage.

Thirteen

In Search of Daily Bread

One huge obstacle stood in the way of our crazy dream. It was as ominous as a line of Bradley Fighting Vehicles. I could see no way to push through the blockade, and it occupied my thoughts all through the first half of 1997.

How in the world were we going to pay the bills?

The United States Army certainly wouldn't be floating my seminary expedition. I'd be leaving active duty and giving up the comfortable pay and perks of a sergeant first class—from free housing to free medical care to shopping at PX prices. Instead, I would be taking a wife and two little sons—plus another one on the way—off to a strange city with no connections or job in sight.

I figured I could work the overnight shift at UPS or FedEx, tossing boxes to make ends meet. Of course eventually I would wear down under the load of daytime classes. Or Dawn could go out, after the baby was born, and get a good secretarial job like she had before; her skills were excellent. But that would seriously shortchange the boys. We just did not want to do that. They needed their mom full time.

So what else? I wrestled with this problem every day. I prayed about it. Dawn and I talked nearly every night. We knew in our minds that God would provide for his calling, but we certainly couldn't see how that was going to take shape in our case.

One morning in the dining facility, I happened to spot an unexpected face—my friend Kurt Smith. "Kurt!" I called across the tables. "What are you doing here?"

"Just down for some training," he called back. He was in a different job now. "I'll save you a place!"

At the table over a hearty collection of boiled eggs, bagels, cereal, cereal bars, and orange juice, we had a great time catching up with each other's lives. I soon said, "Hey, Kurt, you know me. You know about my faith. Well, guess what I'm planning to do next? This fall I'm going to start seminary! Wild, huh?"

"Man, that's great!" Kurt replied. "Where are you headed?"

I described our hopes for relocating to Louisville. But I also confessed I didn't know how I was going to make this work financially.

"Well, have you thought about . . ." He began reeling off options. Some I had already considered; others were new. But all of them had complications. We kept talking for close to an hour. In the end we struck out on every possibility.

"I don't know, man," he said, looking me in the eye. "But I'll tell you this much: if God is calling you to the ministry, he'll take care of you somehow. I really believe that."

I did, too. I was just getting anxious for God to roll out the specifics.

A couple of days later, I was talking with a group of senior NCOs. As usual the topic was my bizarre notion of leaving the army for seminary. One fellow, Master Sergeant Bill Bunnell, was a Christian for whom I had worked a couple of times.

"Hey, Jeff," he said, "when you get up there, why don't you go to ROTC? You might get one of those Green-to-Gold Scholarships for enlisted guys who want to further their education. And when you finish, you'd be a second lieutenant. Just about every school has ROTC."

I thought that was one of the dumber ideas I had heard. ROTC at a *seminary?* Not a chance. "From what I've heard, seminaries don't even particularly *like* soldiers," I shot back. "They're sure not going to have an ROTC program."

"Well, okay," he answered. "I'm just trying to help you with some advice."

"Thanks, Sergeant," I said. "But it's not going to work."

A Glimmer to Pursue

If I wasn't teaching an RIP class, my normal routine in the early morning was to run four to six miles. If I had a lot on my mind, however, and needed time to mull things over, I would extend that to ten, twelve, or fourteen miles. It was my way of concentrating. I would think and pray as I ran.

One morning while it was still dark, I was wandering through Fort Benning, obsessed as usual with my financial problem. *God, what am I going to do about this? I really need an answer of some kind. I can't just take Dawn and the kids up there with no job. This isn't working . . .*

In that moment, as I was running down the shadowy road, a light went on in my brain. *How about getting a job teaching ROTC at a school close to the seminary?*

Wow. This could work! I felt it was a brainstorm from heaven that might actually be practical.

As soon as I got to my desk that morning, I went on-line looking for ROTC programs near Louisville. I also checked out the Wake Forest–Raleigh–Durham area of North Carolina, which would allow me to go to Southeastern Baptist Seminary instead. I began making phone calls from the list I made.

I knew this was not the norm. Army guys—especially enlisted—generally don't go job hunting. The army tells *you* what to do next, not the other way around.

But I thought it wouldn't hurt to try. I started for some reason with the North Carolina schools, saying, "Hello, I'm Sergeant First Class Jeff Struecker in the Third Ranger Battalion, Fort Benning, and I was just wondering, does your ROTC faculty have any openings?"

North Carolina State said no. Duke said no. The University of North Carolina said no.

Later in the day, I dialed the University of Louisville. A guy named Don Coder answered the phone. I gave him my brief little spiel—and the first words out of his mouth were these: "How soon can you get here?"

What? He's kidding, right?

"Well, this summer for sure," I answered, trying to control my excitement. "Why? What's up?"

"I'm at twenty years, and I'm retiring in the next six months. We've been looking for the right person here to replace me for a long time, and we still don't have him. If we don't get somebody, they're not going to let me retire."

"Maybe this is your answer!" I said. "Let me tell you a little about myself." I then launched into my resume in the army. At the end I concluded with, "And I'm really interested in this assignment."

There was a pause. "I don't think that's going to work."

"Why not?"

"This is a mechanized position, and you're a light-infantry guy. We couldn't hire you if we wanted to."

The difference between these two backgrounds would not matter in the least when it came to the real task of training college students to be army officers. ROTC curriculum is generic, covering every job specialty in the army. This was just a kink in the bureaucracy that said the last instructor had a mechanized-armament history, so the next guy should, too.

"Look, Sergeant—who do I need to talk to in order to get this job?" I persevered.

"Not me, not the battalion commander, not even the regimental commander," Don Coder replied. "The only person who can put you in this job is sitting in Washington, D.C., right now. Her name is Staff Sergeant Terry Foxx. She's the key to all ROTC assignments in the United States Army."

"Thanks," I said and quickly hung up.

That reminded me of someone else in D.C.—a friend we all called "Duke" (his last name was Durken), who handled all Ranger assignments. I quickly called him.

"Hey, Duke, I need your help!" I said. "I want an ROTC teaching assignment, specifically the one that's coming open at the University of Louisville. What do you think you can do for me, man?"

He punched at his computer for a few minutes and then said, "Won't work. You're a dismounted infantryman, and that slot is mechanized. How about Bowling Green, Kentucky, instead? Or how about one of the Nashville schools? I can do those for you."

I was disappointed again. I said, "No, thanks, but say, do you know

Staff Sergeant Terry Foxx? She's in assignments like you, right? What's her phone number?"

He looked up the number and dictated it to me. "But it's not going to do you any good," he warned. "Sorry about that."

I wasn't going to believe him. About a half hour later, I dialed Staff Sergeant Foxx.

"Hello. My name is Sergeant First Class Jeff Struecker at Third Ranger Battalion, Fort Benning . . ." I went on with my information. "I want to replace Sergeant First Class Don Coder at the University of Louisville. Would you make the necessary arrangements to put me in that assignment?"

Once again I hit the bureaucratic wall. "Nope, sorry, can't do that. We need a mechanized person for that slot."

"Look, he is retiring, and they don't have anybody to take his place. They're really looking for people . . ."

She cut me off. "I'm really sorry, Sergeant. We jump the track like you're asking only about 1 percent of the time. And the only person who could approve this is my boss. He's a colonel. It would take me going into his office and pleading on your behalf for this job."

I begged her to intercede with the colonel. I wouldn't let go. I did everything I could think of to keep her on the line.

Eventually she started to sound exasperated. "Why do you want this job so badly, anyway?" she asked.

I thought to myself, *Oh, boy, here we go. This is going to get ugly.*

At that very instant, something clicked in her mind. "Wait a minute," she said. "You said your name was—are you the Jeff Struecker who won Best Ranger a year ago?"

"Well, yes, I am," I replied. "I had a very good partner."

I could tell she was now getting confused. "So why on earth do you want this job?" she shot back. "It's not a high-speed assignment at all for somebody like you."

There was no more hiding the facts. I gulped and then said, "To be honest with you, I'm a Christian. I feel very strongly that God has called me to the ministry. There's a seminary on the other side of Louisville that I want to go to. That's why I want the job."

"Oh, praise God!" she exclaimed. "Why didn't you say so at the beginning? What's your Social Security number? Let me put you on hold while I go in and talk to my boss!"

Tottering on the Edge

I sat there holding a quiet phone for the next forty-five minutes. I vacillated between excitement and despair. More than once I thought she had totally abandoned me and I should just hang up. But what would it hurt to wait just a few more minutes? I hung on.

At last she returned to the phone. "Well, Sergeant," she announced, "I talked to the colonel, and he's not very happy about this. But he's willing to do it if a couple of other pieces fall into place. Let me get a little more information from you." She proceeded to ask two more questions, and then the call ended. She never did confirm that I would get the job.

What else could I do to help matters in the meantime?

The next day I decided to see my command sergeant major, Mike Hall, again. After all, he had offered to help me when I first told him of my plans. He would have to sign the paperwork for any ultimate change.

"Sergeant Major Hall, I need your help," I announced after knocking on his door. I told him about the job at the University of Louisville and summarized my steps to get it up to this point. "Nobody is really saying I can have this yet. Do you think you can pull any strings for me?"

"I know the command sergeant major of ROTC," Mike replied. "Let me call him." He placed the call and began talking to the man. The answer, as so many times before, was no.

He then tried Duke, the Ranger assignments guy whom I had already approached. No luck there. Mike tried somebody else he thought might be able to help, only to be turned down.

At this point he turned to his computer and began searching the personnel database. He studied the screen for several minutes. Finally without looking my way, he pronounced the most crushing words I could imagine: "Jeff, you can't have that job. It's already filled. It's gone."

No! As of last night, I had some glimmer of hope from Staff Sergeant Foxx. And now within twelve hours, the job was no longer open? I could not believe it. How could this have happened?

"Sergeant Major, could you just check and see who they filled the assignment with?" I was thinking, *I'll call the guy up and offer to trade with him. Whatever he wants in the army, I'll go get it, and then we can swap.*

"Okay, hold on." I could tell Mike was getting frustrated with all my requests.

He tapped at his computer for a bit longer. Eventually he said, "Here's the Social Security number of the person . . . ," and when he read out the number, it was mine! Apparently Staff Sergeant Foxx had already plugged me into this position without yet notifying me.

It was as if God were saying, *Here you go, Jeff. You wanted this job, and so I'm giving you the desire of your heart.* At the end of all this contacting and inquiring and badgering, my financial dilemma was finally being laid to rest.

One Last Hurdle

Well, not quite at the end. I still had to sell myself to the ROTC commander in Louisville. Just because the Pentagon said he would be getting Jeff Struecker on his faculty didn't mean he had to agree. He was, after all, a lieutenant colonel. His name was Robert Lesson.

I opted once again to take the initiative, even though I was a lowly NCO. I dialed his number and introduced myself. I summarized my qualifications. Without telling him that I'd already been assigned to his unit, I said, "Sir, I've talked with Sergeant First Class Don Coder and heard about his retirement plans. I'd like to replace him."

"Well, send me your bio, and I'll take a look at it," he said. "Then call me back at this time tomorrow."

I faxed him my bio. I could hardly sleep that night for the anticipation of what the next day would bring.

When I called him back, he said, "I was very impressed by your bio. You've done a lot of good things in the army. However, my staff and I have some serious reservations about hiring you."

"What's the problem, sir?" I asked. "What is it that's a concern for you?"

"Well, ROTC works with college students, as you know. We really have to be flexible in dealing with their issues and complexities. You've done too many high-speed, hardcore things in your career. It's just not a good fit." (I found out later that he had made copies of my resume for his entire teaching staff, and they were unanimous that a Ranger would be too intense for ROTC. One of them even said, "Sir, you'll kill the program if you hire this guy. He'll drive everybody off.")

I had to mount a defense, and do it quickly. "Sir, if I may be honest with you," I began, "I've been an RIP instructor for the past three years. What that simply entails is training privates for the Ranger Regiment. These guys are like your students; they're not all that far out of high school. They bring the same problems, the same concerns, the same immaturity that you face there at the university. If I can work with these guys and prepare them for service as Rangers, I can work with college students. I know I can."

Lieutenant Colonel Lesson did not rebut what I said. He asked another couple of questions. Then he came around to the one I'd already heard several times: "Tell me—why do you want this job?"

By now, my reply was virtually memorized. I had found the courage to give it several times already, and it hadn't backfired yet. So I plunged in. "Sir, there's a seminary across your town that I want to attend . . ." I told him I would work tirelessly for him throughout the days if I could go to seminary on nights and weekends.

"All right," he said at last. "Against the advice of all the officers on my staff—you're hired. How soon can you get here?"

The last hurdle had been bridged. I had a way to support my family while training for the ministry. God had heard our anxious prayers and provided a solution. We could head for Louisville at last.

The Grind—and Beyond

The three-and-a-half years to a master of divinity degree were demanding. I functioned on less sleep than ever before. In addition to ROTC responsibilities and seminary work, Dawn and I agreed to lead the youth ministry at a church in exchange for free housing. Our son Joseph was born just after we arrived in town, and Abigail joined us in April 1999.

By early 2000 Dawn was reaching her limit. She sat me down for a talk one Saturday morning. "I don't think I can keep taking this," she announced. "You go to work in the morning, you stay in the city for class at night, you come home late and say hello, then you go right to homework, you sleep for a couple of hours, and you're out the door the next morning to start all over again. On the weekends, we have to be with the teenagers. Something has to change."

"I hear you," I replied. "I'm really strung out myself. What are we going to give up?"

We talked through the options. Quit seminary this close to the end? That didn't make sense. Quit the church job? We'd have to find another place to live, which would cost more money—and would also cut off our practical ministry experience, which was important for whenever we started applying for full-time church positions.

The least of the evils seemed to be to resign from teaching ROTC. Yes, that would cut off our main paycheck. But maybe I could pick up an interim pastor position until school was finished. This would be a new level of trust in God to supply our financial needs, for sure.

I put in the paperwork to quit the army for the sake of my wife and children. Lieutenant Colonel Lesson told me I was pretty much crazy, and I told him I realized that, but my family came ahead of my career. He and other military people kept talking to me about various creative options, and one proved to be worthwhile. I could become a chaplain, conducting services for the troops and counseling them through the many problems and stresses of their lives that

I knew so well from firsthand experience. My "congregation" would be soldiers and their families. My background could be put to a whole new use.

On April 16, 2000, at five o'clock in the evening, I mustered out of the United States Army. At nine o'clock the next morning, I *rejoined* the army in the chaplain candidate program. This was an unpaid position that made me promise I would become a chaplain either in the reserves, the National Guard, or on active duty as soon as I finished seminary in December. Meanwhile, I was named an officer as a second lieutenant.

For the next eight months, we lived on a tiny amount of income from interim pastoring—so small that the IRS audited us the following year, not believing that a family of six could make it on that figure. But we did. I used up every bit of my GI Bill that I could to pay tuition. God provided in amazing ways.

I graduated from seminary debt free. In January 2001 I reported to Fort Jackson, South Carolina, for thirteen weeks of chaplaincy training, and in March we took up our first chaplaincy assignment with the Eighty-second Airborne Division at Fort Bragg, North Carolina. We ministered there for two-and-a-half years. Our youngest child, Lydia, was born during this stint.

Then I asked the army, in view of my history, to consider placing me with a Ranger unit. That moved us across the country to Fort Lewis, Washington, the headquarters of the Second Ranger Battalion. What started as a flickering dream in the ashes of Mogadishu now became a full-time calling, thanks to the grace and provision of an all-wise God. He made a way, he saw that the bills got paid, and he gave a platform to guide young Rangers toward the Savior. For all this Dawn and I were truly grateful.

Fourteen

On Edge

BY THE TIME THIS BOOK GETS READY FOR THE PRINTER, I will be back in the Middle East for the sixth time since the War on Terror began following 9/11. My Ranger battalion will be called upon once again to take the fight to the enemy, and as their chaplain, I go wherever they go. I jump where they jump, eat what they eat, sleep where they sleep, and encourage them every chance I get.

Much of what we'll be doing is classified; I can't describe it for you in the midst of an ongoing war. Even my wife won't know ahead of time. That's the nature of Ranger missions. We move silently, lightning fast, and let everybody figure it out later.

I can, however, give you a couple of snapshots from past incursions. These will show you what it's like to face your fears on today's kind of battlefield.

WAITING FOR THE ROCKETS

In the spring of 2004, I was spending a few days with a small group of our guys at a bleak desert location just inside Afghanistan, along the Pakistani border—basically, Osama bin Laden's neighborhood. This fire base was about as austere as it gets. Rolls of concertina wire marked off a space no more than two hundred yards by three hundred yards. High mountains surrounded us on all sides, and we knew they were full of Taliban fighters. I invited a Catholic priest to go with me, so we each could minister to our respective soldiers.

"Is it safe up there?" he asked me apprehensively. He was a reserve chaplain who just recently had been called into active duty.

"Who knows?" I answered. "Don't worry about it. I'll take care of you. You can count on me to get you back in one piece, okay?"

Now as the sun went down this day, we had just concluded services for the men—he in one corner of the camp with the Catholic guys, me in another corner with the Protestants. I was milling around talking to soldiers in my group before they went back to their responsibilities for the night, asking them how they were doing, seeing who had gotten recent word from their family back home, and simply being available. That's a big part of what any chaplain does. You never know when somebody will ask to talk to you about a spiritual concern.

Suddenly without warning—*whoooooosh!* The distinctive sound of a Russian-made 107-millimeter rocket filled the air. I knew in an instant what it was; these things make a noise in flight like none other. They're about the size of a small melon, can travel as far as ten kilometers, and they cover quite a radius when they burst.

"Get down!" I yelled. Everybody hit the deck. We waited—until *kaboom!* The rocket detonated several hundred yards short of us.

"Okay, that was thrilling," somebody wisecracked as we stood back up again and dusted ourselves off. We could tell the rocket came from very near the border.

Just then the priest came running toward me. I urged him to go inside the little tent where he had put down his gear. "Just wait it out there," I said. "We'll be okay."

He did as I instructed and had just arrived at his destination when—*whoooooosh!* Here came a second rocket. Those of us who had experienced this kind of ammo before could tell by the sound that it was going to hit closer this time. In fact it did—less than a football field away from us, still on the short side.

The joking stopped. Somebody was definitely out to do us harm. The priest stuck his head out of the tent, eyes wide.

"You two guys!" I called to two soldiers nearby. "Grab the priest and whoever else isn't essential right now, and put 'em inside the bunker!" This was a rough set of two walls made of dirt and sand stacked up inside wire frames, with a metal sheet for a roof onto which we had shoveled more mud and dirt. They'd be safe there unless a rocket landed directly on the roof or at one of the two ends. If that ever happened, you'd know it was your time to die.

Meanwhile, I kept walking around in the open, making sure everybody with a clear assignment was doing it, and trying to bolster confidence. I spotted three men who didn't have jobs at the moment; they were huddling near a mud-brick building. "You might want to just go inside and wait this out," I said to them. They nodded and started to move toward the door.

Then one looked back at me. "Well, what about you, Chaplain?" he asked.

"What do you mean?"

"Are you coming inside with us?"

"No."

"Why not?"

I decided to tell him the truth. "Because I know where I'm going to spend eternity," I said. "As a matter of fact, if the three of you don't know what's going to happen to you when you die, you might want to go inside there and pray that God gives you another day to figure that out."

The look on their faces said they were not impressed with my suggestion, at least for right now. That was okay; maybe they would think about it later.

Just then—*whooooosh!* Here came rocket number three, and it sounded even closer than the second. I grabbed the man nearest to me and pulled him down alongside me behind a dirt rock wall. We waited.

The rocket zoomed over our heads and landed maybe 150 meters *beyond* us this time. We both knew what this meant. The enemy was "bracketing" us, gradually narrowing their fix on exactly where we were.

Okay, the next one's gonna come right down our throats, I thought. The seriousness of our danger hit me with full force. I had been all macho with the priest, telling him this trip was nothing to sweat. Now I had to admit: *Somebody's going to get killed here tonight. I wonder who it will be?*

Over to one side, our mortar men were feverishly dialing in the coordinates and turning their 81-millimeter tubes in the direction of the incoming blasts. They kept scanning the sky for any sounds or sights that would help them determine where to aim. I ran over to join them.

In that instant, a fourth *whoooosh!* came rising from the east. I looked in the eyes of this mortar team, and in every one I saw the same awful recognition: *Al-Qaeda knows exactly where we are. They've landed short, then landed long—now here it comes—*

It is amazing how much thinking you can do in a split second. The sound of the propellant started to fade as the actual rocket coasted in to explode. In those moments I thought of Dawn and the kids back home. *God, I don't want to leave her to raise five children on her own!* I prayed. *That's way too much to ask of any woman. My family really needs me.*

But then—with the rocket still airborne—my thoughts flew to *Isn't it a little selfish to ask God to spare my life when I'm the unit chaplain? More than any other man here, I know where I'm headed—From an eternal perspective, I shouldn't be the one to shrink from death.*

Okay, I concluded, *if anybody's going to die here tonight, it might as well be me. God, do whatever you think best.*

Boooom! The rocket detonated within fifty feet of my position. The mortar guys and I looked at each other. When we realized we were all still alive and unharmed, we let out sighs of relief. Then they immediately sprang into action, adjusting their angles one last time and firing 81-millimeter rounds into the nighttime sky. They showed awesome courage under fire, as well as proficiency with their weapon system. Their outbound barrage was withering.

Whoever had been firing at us quickly got the message. No more rockets came our way that night. The Catholic priest and I managed to get safely back to base a day or two later. Both of us had seen anew how close heaven can get to earth. Yet we lived to serve another day.

DODGING ROADSIDE BOMBS

More than a year later in a certain city in central Iraq, I faced the same uneasiness again. That's the way it usually is with our fears. We don't beat them back once and for all. They keep returning to test us, to see if we still have the faith and courage we showed last time. If in the interim we loosen our grip on God's steady hand and grow weak, our fears will be more than willing to come and torment us.

We got a tip this particular day that one of the wanted leaders of the insurgency was wounded and recuperating literally within blocks of our Ranger base. Enough people had corroborated the tip that we felt justified in quickly assembling an assault force to go after him. If we could nail this guy, it would go a long way in dampening the fires of unrest across the country.

Captain Wade Bovard, a company commander, was in charge, and since I happened to be there, I asked if I could go along. "Of course, we'd love to have you, Chaplain," he answered.

I didn't stop to think how similar this would be to that day long ago in Mogadishu. But here we were once again, a band of Rangers and others heading into a hostile urban environment to snatch a notorious killer. We didn't have time to line up air support; we needed to get moving within minutes to reach the target building.

The vehicles were in a row with engines already starting when all of a sudden an intelligence analyst came running out from the operations center. "Captain Bovard! Wait!" he yelled. In his hand he waved a map.

"What?" the commander said.

The analyst held up his freshly printed satellite map and said, "You're driving down this road, right?" pointing with his finger. "Then you're turning here, and heading down this second road to the target building. Don't go that way!"

"Why not?" Captain Bovard asked.

"On that second road, you have a 100 percent chance of getting blown up by an IED [improvised explosive device, or roadside bomb]. We chart these kinds of things. I'm serious!"

The captain looked at me a bit dumbfounded, and I looked back at him.

"But if you take this other route," the man continued, "it's only 90 percent. And on this road," he said, pointing again at the map, "it's an 80 percent chance. But on this other road that comes around to the target from the opposite direction, you've got about a 65 percent chance of getting blown up."

Captain Bovard and I looked at each other again and said, "You know, how about if we take the 65 percent road?"

We ordered all the convoy drivers out of their vehicles. We spread out the map on a hood and showed them what we had just learned. "Here's the way we're going to go," Captain Bovard announced. "Forget what we told you earlier. This is our best option."

Soon we headed out the main gate and into the city. I stared straight ahead, thinking about what had just happened. Despite our change of route, I still had a greater than 50/50 chance of getting blown up in the next few minutes. I studied every alley, every intersection, and every pothole in the road. All my senses were on high alert for anything odd or suspicious.

I heard an explosion in the distance. *What was that?* I wondered. I tried to calculate how far away it was.

As the Humvee rolled on, I began thinking about my mortality once again. *IEDs are the biggest killer of Americans in Iraq today,* I reminded myself. *God, please keep this operation safe. Help us get the job done without losing anybody. This is a lethal situation. We need you.*

I was no longer a single twenty-year-old sergeant in Panama—or a twenty-two-year-old staff sergeant in Kuwait—or a twenty-four-year-old squad leader in Somalia. I was now a thirty-six-year-old captain, a chaplain, a husband, and a father of five. I brooded over the many responsibilities I would leave undone if something happened.

Who would little Abigail and Lydia find to tell them they were special and beautiful if I weren't around? Who would walk them down a wedding aisle? How would Aaron, Jacob, and Joseph figure out what it means to be a man without their dad? Who would help Dawn cope with the many challenges of single parenting?

The fear of letting down those who look to you for leadership and support is one of life's most penetrating concerns. It gets right to the core of your being. If you don't believe that your life is in God's hands, and that there is no such thing with him as an "untimely death," you can just about go crazy.

I struggled with this the rest of the ride. I pulled out of it only when we arrived unharmed at the target building. We started to secure the perimeter while another unit rolled up from a different direction. We could tell the men were agitated.

Captain Bovard and I walked over to this group's senior commander. "Hey, what route did you take?" we asked quietly.

He pointed and said, "We just came up that road over there."

"Did anything happen?" I asked.

"Yeah—two IEDs. The first one went off before we reached it, but the second one blew off a tire from one vehicle—and it was supposed to be armored. Nobody got hurt, though."

"We were supposed to go that way, too," Captain Bovard said, "until our intel said it was 100 percent chance of getting blown up."

"Well, it would have been nice to know that!" the other commander said with a faint chuckle.

There was no time for further conversation. Our men moved into action, storming the building. As it turned out we did not get our intended terrorist after all—at least not that day. We drove away empty-handed but determined to be back as soon as the next opportunity presented itself. We were not about to quit drilling just because one hole had come up dry.

Life on edge is not anybody's favorite. The longer we live, the less we relish the idea of risk. We think about all the other components of our life, especially our families, and worry that something is going to disrupt the scene in a major way. We'd much rather keep things on a steady, predictable keel.

The trouble is we lack the power to insure that on our own. As the Bible says, "How do you know what will happen tomorrow? For your life is like the morning fog—it's here a little while, then it's gone" (James 4:14). The only way to keep our heads and stifle our panic in this kind of setting is to trust the One who controls all things. If we have submitted to his leadership, he promises to keep us in his care and to manage the events of our lives for good. He is the ultimate cure for the apprehensions that try to drown us.

Chaplains Jeff Struecker and Chris Dickey.

Fifteen

THE ANCHOR

IF WE WERE HONEST, NEARLY EVERY HUMAN BEING WOULD admit to being afraid of something. We wake up at 2:30 in the morning, and our minds start spiraling as we lie there in the darkness:

What if my son is doing drugs and I don't know it?

What if my teenage daughter gets pregnant?

What if my husband or wife, sleeping right here beside me, sits me down for a talk this weekend and says, "I need to tell you that I've been seeing someone else for the last few months. Our marriage is over; I want a divorce"?

What if the next time I go to the doctor, he comes into the room after some testing and says, "We have a serious problem here. A cancer is growing on your spine"?

What if this Friday the company announces a layoff of three thousand employees—and I'm one of them?

Or on the management side of the business:

What if sales continue to skid, and I can't meet the company's payroll next week? If the bank won't extend our line of credit, will I have to declare bankruptcy?

What if somebody breaks into this house right now and points a gun at my head?

Virtually no one goes through life without asking questions such as these. For some they are a daily torment. I've had to deal with plenty of fears throughout my life, as this book has made plain. Now as a chaplain, I'm often asked how to handle these things.

SUBSTITUTES THAT FAIL

The answer I give depends on who's asking the question. Naturally in my line of work, I talk to a lot of young soldiers every week who are strong, disciplined, highly trained defenders of our nation—but they are not on God's wavelength at all. The thought that God might have a remedy for their secret fears is not at the front of their minds. The only reason some of them even talk to me is because, in some vague notion, they think I might know something about life in general.

They've tried other solutions that didn't turn out so well. Quite a few of them have turned to alcohol to make them feel better, more in control. I'm sorry to say that a few have turned to illegal drugs. Some have looked for casual liaisons on the weekends. What has happened is that they were running from their problems.

Now they've come to realize it's not working. Getting drunk may have put their fears on hold for a few hours, but then they returned. Drugs may have numbed their anxiousness. Waking up in bed with a strange woman may have diverted their attention for a while. But the difficulties are still there, waiting as before.

"Well," I say to my soldiers, "as much as we all like to think we're in total control, the truth is we're not. Stuff happens that our best training and most incredible technology cannot prevent. Your life may end with a bullet in your chest next month—or you may live another fifty years. I don't know. Neither do you.

"But if you have Christ in your life, you cannot lose. No matter the circumstances of your death, you win. You'll be victorious." What I try to do is broaden their outlook from the problem at hand to the larger issues.

Some guys, understandably, wonder if they'll be cheated out of living a full life if they take the gospel seriously. I try to show them that this is a myth. "God is on your side, remember?" I say. "Jesus said he came to earth to bring *abundant* life. Even the rules and guidelines have a purpose to them. They make life better in the long run.

"God isn't trying to spoil our fun. He is seeking to improve our quality of life."

When we reach out in God's direction, he takes us into his circle of love and assurance. We say with David, "My future is in your hands" (Psalm 31:15).

It's the safest place to be.

THE BIG ONE

No doubt the king of all the fears we battle is the fear of death. What's going to happen to us when we die? Not everyone is as paralyzed by this thought as I was while a young boy, but everybody thinks about it.

For the twentieth anniversary of the highly successful television talk show *Larry King Live* in 2005, the well-known host sat in the guest chair for one night, while Barbara Walters interviewed him. They talked about the memorable moments of the past two decades and what had drawn so many millions of viewers since 1985.

Barbara Walters was her usual rapid-fire self, hitting Larry King with a barrage of blunt questions. "Are you very rich?" "Do you wish you could sing?" "What living person do you most admire?" Eventually she came to this one: "What is your greatest fear?"

Larry King did not flinch. Immediately he gave a one-word answer, with all seriousness. "Death."

He did not say, "My greatest fear is that my show might get canceled." He didn't say, "That my ratings might drop." He didn't say, "That my broker might embezzle all my money." No, the thought of dying was worse than any of these to Larry King. Barbara quickly moved to the next question. "Do you believe in God?"

Larry's forthright answer: "Not sure. I'm an agnostic. Don't know."[1]

As soon as I heard that, I thought, *The two answers fit together, don't they?*

To be uncertain about the reality of God leaves a big problem when it comes to death. It means being cast out into a void. You're not sure what or whom to grasp.

But if we know there's a God, and we've come to terms with him by accepting his offer of forgiveness and salvation, we have a certainty about what eternity holds. We know God is there already, and he will welcome us as one of his family.

Sometimes I tell soldiers, "I don't have a bulletproof body, but I do have a bulletproof faith. I have a belief that transcends death. No matter what happens to me here in Iraq or wherever the army sends me, I'm guaranteed an eternity in heaven."

Some of the young eighteen- and nineteen-year-old guys I talk to are not as forthright as Larry King; they won't admit that they are afraid of death. These are the ones who worry me the most. They don't think they're ever going to die. As a result they live as if there's no end in sight. They know they aren't right with God, and they could not care less.

Death is 100 percent certain for everybody on the planet, and there's no vaccine for it. I'm not trying to scare anybody; I'm just stating the fact that an eternity in hell awaits the person who doesn't plan ahead for that day. That ought to be reason to be scared.

Once in a while a brash young soldier comes by and says, "Hey, Chaplain, got a minute? I need your help on something." He proceeds to tell me how he's in some kind of trouble, and the commanding officer is about to come down hard on his misconduct. He wonders if I, as a former enlisted man, would have any ideas to save his neck. "What do you think, Chaplain? Can you give me a tip or something?"

I respond, "I don't know that I have any magic solution to get you off the hook in this present situation. But let's look at a bigger view. Let's talk about changing your life—the way you make decisions, the source of guidance you depend on."

After outlining what it would mean to start a genuine relationship with Christ, I ask if he wants to go this route. Sometimes the guy will say, "Yes, I see what you're talking about. I need that." Others who come to see me, however, will respond, "Chaplain, I'm not a Christian. I know I'm not going to heaven, but frankly, I don't care right now. I enjoy the lifestyle I'm living. In fact, I'll be going out this weekend again to hit the bars and find a woman. I really don't care what you say about that."

"Okay, that's your freedom," I respond, leaning back in my chair. "You get to do whatever you choose to do. Just know that a day will come when you and I and everybody else will have to give an account of everything we did in this life. You might think about what you'll say on that day. Because it's going to happen, whether you want it to or not."

Some will blow off what I say while here in the States, only to come around and talk again when we get to the Middle East and the rockets start flying. I'm glad to talk to them—but even there, I'm always on the lookout for what I call "foxhole faith." Some guys just want to bargain in the face of danger. I try to bring them to embrace real, permanent solutions to the great concerns of life and death, heaven and hell. It doesn't matter if you're in Iraq or Idaho, if you're a soldier or civilian, male or female, young or old—the end is coming for us all, and what we do today in response to Jesus Christ determines the outcome.

ANXIOUS BELIEVERS

On the other hand, I also find myself talking to Christians who are still fearful about the here-and-now, despite having prayed for forgiveness of their sin and having settled the matter of their eternal destinies. Their head tells them that a loving heavenly Father will take care of them. But down in their gut, they are still scared.

I don't condemn this kind of person for being weak or unspiritual, because I've been there too often myself. What I do say, however, is this: *The first thing to grasp is that fear is not a God invention at all.* The Bible says clearly, "God has not given us a spirit of fear and timidity, but of power, love, and self-discipline" (2 Timothy 1:7). The King James Version renders this last term "a sound mind." That is God's ideal for us.

Dozens upon dozens of times, Scripture tells us, "Fear not" or "Do not be afraid." The first occurrence came early in history when God appeared to Abraham, father of the Jewish nation; the last occasions are in the book of Revelation at the very end of the New Testament. In between, angels, prophets, psalm-writers, and Jesus himself repeated the message again and again.[2]

For the Christian this is a great anchor. No matter how difficult the circumstances, you can always count on two facts. One is that God is still in control. He loves you, and he is looking out for your best. Even if you end up walking "through the valley of the shadow of death," God is allowing that in order to mold you into the man or woman he wants you to become. In other words he isn't unnerved by the threats and dangers that stalk us; he instead uses them to make us better people.

I believe part of God's strategy is that the experience of being afraid drives us closer to him. We call out for God's peace, his assurance, and his protection. When I was in Mogadishu that horrible afternoon and night, you better believe I was silently saying, *God, I really need you! This whole thing is spinning out of my control, but I obviously can't leave; I have a job to do. Help me, please. Calm my insides. Keep my head on straight. Help me lead my squad through this nightmare.*

I hope I never get wounded in combat—but if I do, I will call out to God with all my soul, and I believe he will give me the strength to keep doing what he has asked me to do. If I were debilitated permanently in some way, he would continue to stand by me. He would enable me to cope with life in a wheelchair or some other radical limitation.

After all, he has promised, "I will never fail you. I will never forsake you" (Hebrews 13:5). The effect of this promise comes in the next verse. "That is why we can say with confidence, 'The Lord is my helper, so I will not be afraid. What can mere mortals do to me?'" (Hebrews 13:6).

And what if I lost my life altogether?

The other bedrock fact for the believer is that heaven is waiting. The worst possible thing according to earthly standards is the *best* thing that can happen to a Christian. No soldier wants to become a KIA. But if it happens, the consequence on the other side can be fantastic. As the apostle Paul wrote while sitting in a Roman prison: "I live in eager expectation and hope that . . . my life will always honor Christ, whether I live or I die. For to me, living is for Christ, and dying is even better" (Philippians 1:20–21).

Paul's whole life as an apostle was pretty much an extended version of Ranger School, so to speak! Long marches, shipwrecks, sleeping out in the cold, getting chased from one town to another—you name it. Maybe that's why he held a more balanced perspective about death. It would not be the ultimate disaster for him. It would be a promotion.

These facts do not necessarily erase our anxieties, but they do cast them in a broader light. We still have to face our fears head-on. We have to play the hand of cards we've been dealt. We still have to cope with the doctor's diagnosis, and we naturally wonder how much it's going to hurt in the weeks and months ahead.

Along the way, however, we affirm that "God causes everything [even nasty things] to work together for the good of those who love God" (Romans 8:28). He will not abandon us. And if we end up dying, so what? We will have landed in the best situation of all— our heavenly home.

OUT OF HIDING

I know that some people get antsy even talking about being afraid—especially some of us males. We're so locked into our persona as a "man of steel" that we won't let anybody know what's actually scaring us.

I confess I was this way for a long time. I didn't want to admit that fear and pain and suffering are part of being human, just as much as joy and hope and love. I thought it was wrong for a Ranger to show emotion. Whatever was bothering me got stuffed inside. I wouldn't dare let anybody see that I was troubled about something.

There is no such animal as a "man of steel." The guy that never experiences pain or apprehension never walked planet Earth. Every human being is subject to weakness and uncertainty. It is not wrong to express that.

During my first long deployment as a chaplain, I approached Chris Dickey, another chaplain, and said, "You know what? I'm really struggling right now, and I don't know what to do about it."

"What kind of struggle do you mean?" he asked.

"Just with being away so long. I miss Dawn. I miss the kids."

He smiled and said, "Good for you. You're a human being! It's okay to feel badly about this circumstance. It would be wrong for you *not* to struggle with this, pretending that everything was normal when it's not. Now let's look at how Christ will shore you up to get through this."

I've learned that subordinates relate much better to me when I'm not trying to be so stoic. They appreciate knowing that I have to deal with fear just as they do. I'm not saying I would ever want to lose control and fall apart in front of them, but it is all right to be human and honest about what's bothering me. They see what I'm battling, and that opens the door for them to see how Christ upholds an ordinary human being.

This is not to say that a soldier—or anyone else—doesn't need to be tough. I fully agree with the apostle Paul's words to young Timothy, and quote them often in my messages:

Be strong with the special favor God gives you in Christ Jesus . . . Endure suffering along with me, as a good soldier of Christ Jesus. And as Christ's soldier, do not let yourself become tied up in the affairs of this life, for then you cannot satisfy the one who has enlisted you in his army. (2 Timothy 2:1, 3–4)

But that does not mean you can't admit to the reality of disappointments, struggles, and fears. The more you stuff these things into the dark corners of your soul and refuse to face them, the more unhealthy you become, and the more those around you—employees, spouses, children, assorted friends—find you to be unreal.

Far better to cast your fears upon the Lord, who created you in the first place and loves you to this day with an enduring affection. He is the one who provides your anchor when everything else is churning. The Bible says:

God is love, and he who abides in love abides in God, and God in him. Love has been perfected among us in this: that we may have boldness in the day of judgment; because as He is, so are we in this world. There is no fear in love; but perfect love casts out fear, because fear involves torment. But he who fears has not been made perfect in love. (1 John 4:16–18 NKJV)

The torment of fear is neutralized by the love of God. He gives us the "sound mind" mentioned earlier to keep our equilibrium and know that he is always watching over us. He has not been distracted from our dilemmas. He knows exactly what we're going through.

When I was a young soldier scared to death of flunking out of Ranger School, God was fully aware. He were right on top of the situation, waiting for me to ask for his help. He also saw me that Christmas Eve on the hilltop in Panama, wondering if I was about to be overrun by hordes of Noriega's militiamen. My subsequent worries about dishonoring the name of Christ in front of other soldiers . . . my fear of losing face in the regiment by going into the ministry . . . my struggles to pay the bills during seminary . . . my ever-present risk, even now, of going on a military mission and not coming home again—these dangers are real, and I can cope with them only through God's provision.

He is the One who assures us that if we place our confidence in his wisdom and intelligence, we'll make it after all. He is our ultimate strength, our rock, and our shelter. We'll never find a better solution to our fear than him. If we forget about the anchors of his love for us, his promise to hear our prayers, and the heavenly future that awaits us, we will wallow in our apprehensions like everyone else. But if we hold on to what we know is true, we can live above our fears. As the psalmist put it so well:

When I am afraid,
    I put my trust in you.
O God, I praise your word.
    I trust in God, so why should I be afraid?
    What can mere mortals do to me?
(Ps. 56:3–4)

ENDNOTES

CHAPTER 10

1. "The Life of King Henry the Fifth" in *The Complete Works of William Shakespeare*, ed. W.J. Craig (London: Oxford University Press, 1914; Bartleby.com, 2000), 4.3.40–56, 61–72. http://www.bartleby.com/70/21/7/2006.
2. Irving Berlin, "God Bless America," 1918.
3. Mark Bowden, *Black Hawk Down* (New York: Penguin, 1999), 342.

CHAPTER 15

1. Larry King, interview by Barbara Walters, *Larry King Live*, June 3, 2005, http://transcripts.cnn.com/TRANSCRIPTS/0506/03/lkl.01.html.
2. A sampling of "fear not" Scriptures:
   Genesis 15:1; 21:17; 46:3
   Exodus 14:13; 20:20
   Numbers 14:9; 21:34

Deuteronomy 1:21; 3:2, 22; 20:3; 31:6, 8

Joshua 8:1; 10:8, 25

Judges 6:23

1 Samuel 12:20; 23:17

1 Kings 17:13

2 Kings 6:16

1 Chronicles 28:20

2 Chronicles 20:17

Isaiah 7:4; 35:4; 41:10, 13–14; 43:1, 5; 44:2, 8; 51:7; 54:4, 14

Jeremiah 30:10; 46:27–28

Lamentations 3:57

Ezekiel 3:9

Daniel 10:12, 19

Joel 2:21

Zechariah 8:13, 15

Matthew 1:20; 10:26–31; 28:5

Luke 1:13, 30; 2:10; 5:10; 8:50; 12:7; 12:32

John 12:15

Acts 27:24

Hebrews 13:6

Revelation 1:17; 2:10